Mark Mabry

About the Author

JOHN GRAY, Ph.D., is an internationally recognized expert in the fields of communication and relationships. The author of fifteen books, he has been conducting personal-growth seminars for more than thirty years and writes "Mars Venus Advice," a weekly syndicated column that has appeared in more than one hundred media outlets, including *Newsday*, the *Los Angeles Times*, and the *Detroit Free Press*. He also has a weekly Internet broadcast with more than two million listeners at Marsvenus.com. Gray has been a contributing editor at *Redbook* and a contributor to ivillage. com, *Brides*, and *Divorce* magazine. He lives with his wife and three children in northern California.

WHY MARS & VENUS COLLIDE

WHY
MARS &
VENUS
COLLIDE

**Improving Relationships by Understanding
How Men and Women Cope Differently with Stress**

JOHN GRAY, PH.D.

HARPER

NEW YORK • LONDON • TORONTO • SYDNEY

HARPER

FIRST HARPER PAPERBACK EDITION PUBLISHED 2009.

Designed by Jaime Putorti

Library of Congress Cataloging-in-Publication Data is available upon request.

ISBN 978-0-06-124297-7

15 16 17 18 WBT/RRD 20 19 18 17 16 15 14 13 12

*This book is dedicated with deepest love and affection
to my wife, Bonnie Gray.
Her love has supported me to be the best I can be
and share with others what we have learned together.*

CONTENTS

CONTENTS

ACKNOWLEDGMENTS

I thank my wife, Bonnie, for sharing the journey of developing this book with me. She has been a great teacher as well as my biggest fan. She is a tremendous source of insight, and her capacity to love is a great inspiration. I thank her for expanding my ability to understand and honor the female point of view. This perspective has not only enriched our life together but also provides the foundation for the many insights in this book.

I thank our three daughters—Shannon and her husband, Jon Myers; Juliet and her husband, Dan Levinson; and Lauren—for their continuous love and support. Our many conversations have definitely enriched my perspective on what it means to be a young woman today. The love we share and the many challenges they have each overcome have helped anchor the many practical ideas in *Why Mars and Venus Collide.* I also thank our new grandchild Sophia Rose for the new grace and delight she has brought to our family.

I thank my staff and team, Bonnie Gray, Juliet Levinson, Jeff Owens, Melanie Gorman, Dean Levin, Neil Dickens, Ellie Coren, and Sherrie Natrass for their consistant support and hard work in organizing and producing my talks, seminars, columns, TV show, radio show, infomercial, nutritional product development and distribution, MarsVenus.com Web site, AskMarsVenus.com telephone coaching, MarsVenusDating.com, Mars Venus Coaching training program, MarsVenusGoCleanse.com, and Mars Venus Wellness Retreats. For a small group of people, you do a lot. I also want to thank the hundreds of supportive people who help our team bring this message to the world.

I thank my editors, Kathryn Huck and Diane Reverand, for their brilliant feedback, advice, and editorial expertise, and the CEO of HarperCollins, Jane Friedman, and publisher Jonathan Burnham for their vision and encouragement. I thank Steven Kunkes, M.D., for reviewing the scientific chapters to make sure I had it all right.

The ideas in this book are certainly inspired by my own personal experiences in creating a loving relationship and in helping others do the same, but without the thousands of people who have generously shared their insights, experiences, and research it could never have been so rich. Each page has some jewel of wisdom that I have cherished hearing, and I know you, the reader, will as well. To gather these ideas, it has taken a team of dedicated health, happiness, and relationship teachers, writers, coaches, researchers, therapists, doctors, nurses, patients, and seminar participants over thirty years to refine and develop. Much of this work in developing the new ideas of *Why Mars and Venus Collide* was done through special gatherings and seminars at the Mars Venus Wellness Center in northern California during the past five years.

I thank the colleagues and experts who have aided me during my research: Dr. Daniel G. Amen, John and Cher Anderson, Jack Canfield, Warren Farrell, Jim and Kathy Cover, Tony and Randi Escobar, Dr. Solar Farahmand, Dr. Mitzi Gold, Dr. Dennis Harper, Dr. William Hitt, Peter and Sarah Greenwall, Dr. Tom McNeillis, Dr. Gary Gordon, Ron Reid, Dr. Brian Turner, Harv Ecker, and Dr. Cynthia Watson.

I thank the thousands of people who have shared their personal experiences, concerns, and comments. Their enthusiasm with this material has motivated me and given me the confidence to write this book.

I thank my many friends and family members for their support and helpful suggestions: Robert Gray, Tom Gray, David Gray, and Virginia Gray, Darren and Jackie Stephens, Clifford McGuire, Ian and Ellen Coren, Martin and Josie Brown, Andrea and Reggie Henkart, Mirra Rose, Lee Shapiro, Gary Quinton, Russ and Carol Burns, Rhonda Collier, Rami El Batrawi, Sherrie Bettie, Max and Karen Langenburg, and Malcolm Johns.

I thank my parents, Virginia and David Gray, for all their love and support, and Lucille Brixey, who was always like a second mother to me. Although they are no longer here, their love and encouragement continue to surround and bless me.

INTRODUCTION

In the last fifty years, life has become more complicated. Longer working hours, intensified by grueling commutes and more traffic, the increased cost of housing, food, and health care, rising credit card debt, and the combined responsibilities of work and child care in two-career families are only a few of the sources of stress in our fast-paced modern lives. In spite of the new technologies designed to connect us, information overload and round-the-clock accessibility via the Internet and cell phones have reduced much of our communication to the equivalent of text messaging. We are stretched to the limit, with little energy for our personal lives. Despite increased independence and opportunities for success at work, we are often left with a sense of isolation and exhaustion at home.

The unprecedented levels of stress both men and women are experiencing is taking a toll on our romantic relationships. Whether single or in committed relationships, we are often too busy or too tired to sustain feelings of attraction, motivation, and affection. Everyday stress drains our energy and patience and leaves us feeling too exhausted or overwhelmed to enjoy and support each other.

We are often too busy to see what is obvious. A man will give his heart and soul to make enough money to provide for his family and return home too tired even to talk with them. A woman will give and give to support her husband and children and then resent them for not giving back the kind of support she thrives on giving. Under the influence of stress, men and women forget why we do what we do.

As I travel the world, teaching the Mars and Venus insights, I have witnessed a new trend in relationships linked to increasing stress. Both couples and singles believe they are too busy or too exhausted to resolve their relationship issues, and often think their partners are either too demanding or just too different to understand. Attempting to cope with the increasing stress of working for a living, both men and women feel neglected at home. While some couples experience increasing tension, others have just given up, sweeping their emotional needs under the carpet. They may get along, but the passion is gone.

Men and women have always had challenges in their relationships, but with the added stress of our modern lifestyles, these challenges have become bigger. With increasing stress in the outside world, our needs at home have dramatically changed. Without an understanding of our partners' new needs for coping with stress, we can actually make things worse while trying to make things better.

Fortunately, there is a new way to understand and cope with rising stress levels. Instead of being another problem we have to solve, relationships can actually be the solution. Instead of coming home to a new set of problems and stress, coming home can be a safe haven of loving support and comfort. Understanding how men and women cope with stress in different ways gives us a whole new perspective for improving communication and successfully giving and receiving support in our relationships.

Good communication skills can bring men and women together, but when the increasing stress of our busy lives is added to the mix,

Mars and Venus collide. Stress is a major contributor to why we fight, but the fact that men and women cope with stress differently is at the root of our conflicts. Though men and women are similar, when it comes to stress, they are very different. With increasing stress, these differences are intensified. Instead of facing life's challenges and growing together in love, many couples drift apart to a comfortable but passionless distance, or are ripped apart by feelings of resentment, confusion, and mistrust that lead to explosive fights.

It is sometimes as if we are from completely different planets; men are from Mars and women are from Venus. Without a positive way to understand our different coping mechanisms, Mars and Venus collide instead of coming together.

Men and women not only respond to stress in unique ways, but the kind of support they need to relieve their stress is different as well. In every chapter of *Why Mars and Venus Collide,* we will explore the different ways men and women experience stress as well as the best ways to cope and support each other. My goal in writing the book is to provide you with a new way to understand each other and more effective strategies to create a healthy and happy relationship that will actually lower your stress levels.

The more aware we are of our natural differences, the more tolerant we become when and if those differences show up. Instead of thinking, What's wrong with my partner? you are able to ponder what is wrong with the way you are approaching her. Instead of concluding that your partner is purposefully being inconsiderate, you can at least feel some comfort knowing that he is oblivious or clueless. Couples often have no real sense of how things affect each of them.

Accepting our differences can immediately lighten up our relationships. Many couples feel a heaviness in their lives, because they believe they have to sacrifice themselves to please their partners. This attitude needs to change.

Certainly every relationship requires making adjustments, compromises, and sacrifices, but we do not have to give up ourselves. Instead, we can arrive at a reasonable and fair compromise. Life is not about having everything our own way whenever we want it. We experience the opening of our hearts when we share.

When a plane takes off and flies on automatic pilot, it will arrive at its destination. Though the course seems perfect, it is not. At every point on its route, a plane's course varies due to changing wind speeds and plane resistance. It is never perfectly on target, but it is generally moving in the right direction. A plane on automatic pilot constantly makes small adjustments to correct the direction.

Relationships are the same way. No one is ever perfect, but your partner can be the perfect person for you. If we continue to correct and adjust ourselves, we can create a lifetime of love. When we can own our mistakes and adjust our actions, we can reduce the tension in our relationships.

Without an understanding of our different needs, men and women are adjusting their actions and reactions to no avail. Our actions may be pointed in the wrong direction. My aim in *Why Mars and Venus Collide* is to give you the understanding and the techniques you will need to counter the disruptive effects of stress and to steer a true course to a lifetime of love.

We'll begin by examining the dramatic new source of stress in our lives brought on by the shift in the roles of men and women. The increased pressure on women to work outside the home and the diminished potential of men to earn enough to be sole providers has shaken the foundations of our society. The complex mosaic of traditional roles and expectations for men and women, fashioned and refined for thousands of years, has been shattered, and we are still picking up the pieces.

Never before in history have we witnessed so much social change in such a short period of time. With equal rights, higher education, sexual liberation, and greater financial independence, women today have more choices to create a better life than ever before, but we are all more stressed at home. Never in history have women been expected to do so much, and that can be overwhelming on Venus. Of course, that stress is immediately transmitted to Mars and ends in misunderstanding, friction, and a sense of helplessness.

After looking at the change in the expectations in our relationships, we will review groundbreaking scientific research that supports the gender differences I have described anecdotally in all of my books. There are physiological reasons that women find comfort in talking about their problems and men prefer to retreat, or why women can multitask and remember everything while men focus on one thing at a time, forgetting everything else. I will give you an overview of the scientific research in easy-to-understand terms to show you how the brains and hormones of men and women are hardwired to respond differently to stress.

By examining how we behave differently in stressful situations, a woman's never-ending to-do list, for example, I hope to give you new insights into how our diverse responses to stress cause us to clash. You will see how men and women really are different throughout *Why Mars and Venus Collide*.

Remembering and understanding our differences are only half the battle. The other half is about action—learning to cope more effectively with stress. This book aims to help you discover new ways to lower your own stress and help to lower your partner's. Whether you are in a relationship or single, you will discover a variety of new and practical ways to improve your communication, uplift your mood, increase your energy, elevate levels of attraction in your relationship, create harmony with your partner, and enjoy a lifetime of love and romance. You will learn why communication breaks down or why your relationships have failed in the past, and what you can do now to ensure success in the future.

I will guide you through the anatomy of a fight and give you fail-safe techniques to stop a fight before it becomes hurtful and advice on how to make up. Even more important, I will teach you how to prevent fights from even starting by making Venus Talks a ritual in your lives that will relax Venetians and give Martians a sense of accomplishment with a minimum of effort.

Finally, I will suggest a variety of ways you can reduce stress in relationships by engaging in the world and reaching out to enrich your life. When you learn to cope more effectively with stress and remember the gender differences that are hardwired into our brains, you will blame stress, rather than your partner, for your problems. Instead of waiting for your partner to change, you will learn how to lower your own stress levels. When your stress is reduced, you will be freed from the compulsion to blame or change your partner. Instead, you will remember and experience the pleasure of loving and accepting your partner just the way he or she is, as you did when you first fell in love. Mars and Venus orbit around the sun on their own paths in harmony, just as men and women must do to create lasting love.

For additional support, join millions of others who visit me each week at my Web site, www.marsvenus.com. You can reinforce your new understanding of our differences by watching my free Internet TV show or listening to my radio show. On a regular basis, I answer your online questions on relationships and the biochemisty of health and happiness. In addition, to get extra relationship support regarding your personal situation at any time or place, either planned or when a crisis occurs, you can talk online or by phone with a Mars Venus relationship coach. You can also listen to our regular conference calls, in which I explore many strategies and resources to improve communication, lower stress, and enjoy better health, happiness, and loving relationships.

In addition, I invite you to join the Mars Venus Wellness Community on my Web site, where I give gender-specific advice for healthy nutrition and the cellular cleansing of your body. Just as adjustments in your behavior can make a big difference in lowering your stress levels, small but significant changes in what you eat and how you exercise can make a substantial difference as well.

As you read *Why Mars and Venus Collide,* I hope you share my enthusiasm and begin to talk about these new insights and resources with everyone you know. Together we can create a better world, one relationship at a time.

—*John Gray, Ph.D., April 2007*

WHY MARS & VENUS COLLIDE

CHAPTER ONE

WHY MARS AND VENUS COLLIDE

H ere is a scenario that plays out every night, everywhere:

Susan balances her laptop and the grocery bags she is carrying as she opens the door to the condo she shares with her husband, Marc.

"Hi, sorry I'm late. What a day!" she calls out over the sound of the TV coming from the den.

"Hi, hon," he responds. "I'll be there in a sec. Just want to watch this play."

Susan drops the bags on the counter and begins to sort through the mail Marc left there. She pulls a bottle of water from the refrigerator. "I picked up some salad makings to go with the leftover turkey chili," she calls to Marc, who saunters into the kitchen.

"Oh, I finished the chili when you called to say you'd be late. I was starving." He leans in to give her a kiss. "Are you ready for your presentation?"

"I was looking forward to having it for dinner, before I do more work on the PowerPoint. I don't feel it's as good as it could be. My supervisor is really counting on me. I'm so anxious about this."

"I'm sure it's great! You're overthinking it," he says, trying to reassure her. "You're such a perfectionist."

"Not really. I just don't feel it's right yet. This is really important."

"Maybe we should go out for a bite—it will relax you. I can skip the game."

"Are you kidding? I have too much on my mind, and I want to get a good night's rest."

"Well, we could order in—"

"I'm trying to eat healthy food—pizza won't do it. I'll make scrambled eggs or an omelet and toast. I could use some comfort food."

"Whatever . . ."

"By the way, did you remember to pick up my black pantsuit?"

When she sees Marc's expression, her blood boils. "I can't believe you forgot. I planned to wear that suit tomorrow."

"You have a walk-in closet packed with clothes—"

"That's not the point—I even reminded you."

"Well, I'll get up early and be there when the dry cleaner's opens in the morning—I was too tired to do another thing."

"Just forget it. I want to leave early."

"I'm really sorry, Susan—it slipped my mind."

"Right. Thanks a lot. All I wanted was a little help so I can be prepared for an important day tomorrow."

It is clear from this exchange that the evening ahead will not be relaxing for Susan and Marc, who are headed for a fight. At the very best, they will certainly not be in the mood for romance. What happened between Susan and Marc demonstrates friction points that are common in relationships today. Susan's high-pressure job, her expectations regarding her husband's contribution around the house, his forgetfulness, his dismissal of her anxiety, and his attempt to offer solutions to her problems make for an explosive situation.

As you read *Why Mars and Venus Collide,* you will learn to recognize the assumptions we make every day that fail to take into account how different men and women really are.

We need to challenge our assumptions about how men and women should be and begin to appreciate in practical terms who we are, what we can offer each other, and how we can team up to solve the new problems we face today. We can create a new blueprint for male and female roles that can bring us closer together harmoniously.

Our biggest problem at home is that women expect men to react and behave the way women do, while men continue to misunderstand what women really need. Without a correct and positive understanding of these differences, most couples gradually begin to feel they are on their own rather than relying on the support they felt at the beginning of their relationship.

Women mistakenly expect men to react and behave the
way women do, while men continue to misunderstand
what women really need.

Men love to solve problems, but when their efforts are misdirected and go unappreciated, they lose interest over time. When this challenge is correctly understood, men become much more skillful in helping women cope with the burden of increasing stress in their lives. This book helps to explain this dilemma in a way that most men can understand and appreciate. Even if a woman's partner doesn't read this book, there is still hope. *Why Mars and Venus Collide* is not just about men understanding women. It is also about women understanding themselves and learning how to ask effectively for the support they need. Women will learn new ways to communicate their needs, but more important, women readers will learn how to avoid pushing away the support men already want to give.

Here's another scenario:

Joan is cleaning up the remains of the children's dinner when she hears Steve's car pull into the garage. He comes through the mudroom, having an urgent conversation on his cell phone.

"I can't believe they did that. The papers were supposed to be filed at the end of next week. How are we supposed to pull it together by this Friday? Think we can get an extension until Monday? Do your best. Let me know."

He drops his briefcase and slouches against the counter, ready to check his BlackBerry messages.

"Your day sounds as crazy as mine," Joan says. "Would you like to have some wine? We can sit and talk. So much happened today."

"Wine—er, no," he says, distracted by a text message. "I think I'll just grab a beer and watch the news for a bit."

"I couldn't help overhearing your conversation." Joan pulls a bottle of beer from the refrigerator for Steve. "Does this mean you won't be able to go to Kyle's hockey

tournament this weekend? He'll be so disappointed. And I have to take Melanie to her dance lesson, and Jake to basketball practice and tutoring. I can't be in three places at once."

"I don't want to think about it right now. It might not even be an issue. If we can't get that date postponed, I'll have all the time in the world this weekend, but I'll be a basket case. We'll work it out—don't worry."

"But I have commitments, too. When do you think you'll know?"

"I don't think we can do anything about it until the morning."

"What would you like for dinner? The kids were so ravenous, they devoured the chicken."

"Doesn't matter—whatever you'd like."

"Well, we could have pasta or—"

"Really, Joan," Steve cuts her off. "Whatever you want. I don't want to think about it."

"Lovely—I'm glad you appreciate the meals I shop for and prepare—and I worked today. I'll throw something together for us." She opens a cupboard and surveys its contents. "When we're done, Kyle needs some help with his algebra. His grades are starting to suffer, because he's at practice all the time—"

"All I want to think about now is that soft couch and a droning anchor."

"Dad, you're home!" Little Jake runs into the kitchen with his new basketball. "Want to play catch?"

"Hi, buddy!" Steve greets his son wearily.

"Not now, Jake," Joan says. "Your dad is exhausted. And you should be doing your homework!"

"You guys are never any fun!"

Joan and Steve look at each other and know their son is right. There seems to be no downtime in their lives to kick back and to enjoy the fruits of all their hard work. So many couples today, like Joan and Steve, experience increasing frustration and confusion as they cope with the stress of their day-to-day lives.

In this scenario, rather than considering each other's unique needs to de-stress after a demanding day, Joan and Steve are locked into their own Mars/Venus coping mechanisms, which causes considerable friction between them.

Our Differences Are Intensified by Stress

Relationships are suffering because men and women deal with stress differently. Men are from Mars and women are from Venus, and our differences are intensified by stress. When we do not understand our different coping mechanisms, Mars and Venus collide.

Our greatest challenge today is that men and
women cope with stress differently.

Since men and women do not respond to stress in the same way, the kinds of support we require to relieve stress differ. What helps men release stress can be the opposite of what helps women feel better. While he withdraws into his cave to forget the problems of his day, she wants to interact and discuss things. When she shares her frustrations, he offers solutions, but she is simply looking for some empathy. Without a clear understanding of their unique needs and reactions to stress, they will inevitably feel unsupported and unappreciated. By remembering that men are from

Mars and women are from Venus, we can overcome this tendency to collide and instead come together in mutually supportive ways. Rather than being another source of stress, our relationships can be a safe haven in which we can expect support, comfort, and ease. We need to understand our differences if we are to support each other in overcoming this challenge. This new understanding of how men and women react differently to stress will allow our relationships to thrive rather than just survive.

Recent scientific research, which is covered in the next two chapters, reveals that these different stress reactions are actually hardwired into our brains, and to a great extent are determined by the balance of our hormones. These reactions become more extreme under greater stress. In *Why Mars and Venus Collide,* we will use these scientific insights along with common sense to guide our way. Being aware of our innate biochemical differences frees us from the unhealthy compulsion to change our partners and eventually leads us to celebrate our differences. Instead of resenting each other, we can laugh at our differences. In practical terms, we cannot change the ways our bodies react to stress, but we can change the way we respond to our partner's reactions to stress. Instead of resisting, resenting, or even rejecting our partners, we can learn new ways to provide the support our partners need as well as to get the support we need.

When hopelessness turns back to hope, the love in our hearts can flow again. We all intuitively know that love includes acceptance and forgiveness, but sometimes we just can't find it. With these insights, you will discover a new level of acceptance and love that will transform your life. Instead of trying to change what cannot be changed, you will be able to focus on what is possible to change. In this process, you will discover that you have the power to bring out the best in your partner.

Rather than dwell on what you are not getting or what
you don't want, you will begin to focus on what you
do want and what you can get.

This important shift will provide a new foundation for you to create a lifetime of love. The scenarios in this chapter demonstrate some of the many ways men and women commonly collide. See if you can relate to any of these common complaints or hot spots I hear when counseling both single or married women and men.

COMPLAINTS FROM VENUS	COMPLAINTS FROM MARS
He leaves things all around the house. I am tired of cleaning up after him.	There is always something that I haven't done.
We both go to work. When we get home, why doesn't he pitch in and help more?	She always finds something new to complain about.
He sits in front of the TV while I do everything. I am not his personal maid.	She wants everything done right now. Why can't she just relax?
I can't believe he forgets everything. I can't depend on him for anything that matters to me.	I can't believe she remembers all my mistakes and continues to bring them up.
I have to juggle so many things, and he doesn't seem to care or even want to help.	When I offer to help, she always finds something wrong in my suggestions. Why bother?

COMPLAINTS FROM VENUS	COMPLAINTS FROM MARS
The only time he helps me is when I ask. Why can't he just pitch in like me?	She expects me to be a mind reader and know what she wants.
When I try to talk with him, he is either distracted or he continues to interrupt with solutions.	When I take time to relax or spend time with my friends, she complains that we are not spending enough time together.
When he does talk, he goes on and on and is not interested in what I have to say. I wish he would give me less advice and help more.	I help out around the house, but she is still exhausted. What I do is never acknowledged or appreciated.
He becomes so moody and irritated. I don't know what to do to help. He just shuts me out of his life.	I never know when she is going to erupt with a list of complaints. I feel like I have to walk on eggshells around her.
He used to be more affectionate and interested. Now he ignores me unless he wants something.	She is always complaining about something. Nothing can make her happy.
He doesn't even notice how I look anymore. Is it too much to expect an occasional compliment?	She makes such a big deal out of things. Why does she have to get so emotional?
I can't talk about how I feel and what I think we should do without him feeling as if I am controlling him and telling him what to do.	She either complains that I work too hard, or that we don't have enough money. There is no way I can win.
We never have time for romance anymore. He is either working, watching TV, gone, or sleeping.	When I am in the mood, she is either too tired or overwhelmed with too many other things to do.

(Continued)

COMPLAINTS FROM VENUS	COMPLAINTS FROM MARS
The only time he touches me is when he wants sex.	I feel like I have to jump through hoops to have sex with her.
I spend all day with the kids, and then he comes home and wants to tell me what I do wrong.	When I spend time with the kids, she corrects what I do. She says she wants a break, but then she keeps telling me what to do.
Every time we talk about finances, we get into a fight. What I say doesn't seem to matter.	When we go over the bills, she questions me about the way I spend money. I don't want her telling me what to do.

Do any of these complaints sound familiar? They are only the tip of the iceberg, but they represent a new trend in relationships. If we can see our differences in a new light, we will not only enrich communication in our relationships but also make our relationships a solid base to support all the other areas of our lives. Equipped with new insight, we can actually come closer together while coping with stress instead of being torn apart.

Why We Are Stressed

A dramatic new source of stress in our lives during the past fifty years has been the shift in the roles of men and women. A man used to go to work to provide for his family. The sense of pride and accomplishment he felt, along with the love and support he received when he returned home, helped him to cope with the many stresses of his day.

Women used to spend most of their days creating a beautiful home and family life, while nurturing friends and contributing to the community. Though being a homemaker was demanding, having time to focus on what she had to do enabled a woman to pace her life to minimize stress. There was men's work and women's work. Any additional demands on her partner beyond being a good provider were few, and usually involved heavy lifting.

With today's rising costs, this lifestyle is no longer a choice for all women. More often than not, a woman is expected to contribute financially to provide for a family. At the same time, the women's movement has awakened women and inspired many to find a fulfilling career in order to develop all their talents. When a woman returns home from work feeling responsible for creating a beautiful home and nurturing her family, she has to do this around the demands of her job. This is a new stress, and it requires a new kind of support. No wonder women feel so overwhelmed as they balance the demands of work and home.

Having a job or career is often no longer a choice
for most women, but a necessity.

Men need more support as well. Instead of coming home to rest and recover from a stressful day, a man faces a wife and family who need more from him. His wife expects more help from him to run the household and to participate in their children's busy schedules. No longer enjoying the sense of accomplishment that comes from being a provider, he returns home to his next job. He attempts to provide some measure of support, but he has not had the time he needs to recover from his daily stress. Eventually he, too, becomes tired and irritable. After tending to the many duties of domestic life, there is little time or inclination for couples to concentrate on their relationship. This new male-female dilemma has created an undercurrent of stress that affects all areas of our lives.

Even when a woman chooses to stay at home, she is often too isolated to get the support she needs. More than half of all married women work, and the pool of available friends and organized activities for the nonworking woman has shrunk. In addition, work demands on a man who is the sole supporter of the family are extreme, because raising a family on a single salary has become increasingly difficult. He has neither the time nor energy for his marriage or relationship to be his top priority, to cater to the needs of a partner who seems to be demanding too much of him.

Today, at home we are dealing with the side effects of women becoming more like men in the workplace. Success in the workplace often requires an enormous sacrifice for most women. Without enough time during the day to nurture their feminine side, women commonly become tired, drained, and resentful. At home, natural feelings of comfort, ease, appreciation, and grace are often overshadowed by anxiety, urgency, and exhaustion.

Without new skills for coping with this stress and nurturing their emotional needs, women inevitably expect too much from their male counterparts. This puts an even greater stress on their personal relationships. Habitually and instinctively acting out outdated roles that were created in a far distant past for a different world, both men and women today relate in ways that increase stress rather than lessen it.

Women Want Men to Become Like Women

What we have learned from the workplace is that women can do any job that a man can do. Just because a woman is different and may resolve problems in a unique manner, that does not mean she cannot be just as competent as a man. There is no need for a woman to change who she is to get respect in the workplace or at home.

Being equals does not mean that we have to be the same. To give equal respect, we must recognize that we are different and support those differences. Respect is honoring who a person is and being open to appreciate what he or she has to offer.

Being equals does not mean men and women
are the same or should be the same.

Just as women should not have to change themselves to be respected and appreciated in the workplace, men should not have to change who they are at home. Given their hours working outside the home or the increased demand on them as mothers and homemakers, women undeniably need more help at home, but that need should not require men to change their nature.

In our collective fantasy of an ideal relationship, men still want to return home to a happy partner, who has prepared dinner in their magazine-perfect home and who is responsive to his every sexual desire. Though most women today lack the time, energy, and inclination to live this fantasy, they have their own unrealistic expectations. When women today return home from work, they often wish a loving and supportive wife was there waiting for them.

Women today are so tired and stressed,
they too want a happy wife to greet them at home.

This trend in relationships is creating a new area of conflict. In various ways and to different degrees, women want men to become like women. They want men to share equal responsibility at home and in the relationship. It is no longer enough for a man to be a good provider. If she works outside the home, then to be fair, he should contribute to work inside the home and be more supportive in the relationship. If she is doing traditional "men's work," then he should do traditional "women's work."

This sounds good, but there is another point of view. Just as women want men to change, men want women not to change. Most men, to some degree, want their partners to be the domestic divas their mothers were. A man wants to come home and be supported by his loving wife. Since he is doing what his father did, his wife should do what his mother did. Oblivious to how much it takes to organize a smooth-running household, he expects the impossible from her.

Unrealistic expectations make
changing gender roles nearly impossible.

As men cling to old expectations, women are creating new expectations that are equally unrealistic. To various degrees, women want a sympathetic partner, eager to talk about the stresses of the day, who will share all the domestic responsibilities and duties. She also wants her partner to be attentive and romantic, planning dates for her pleasure after solving the many unscheduled problems and emergencies that inevitably arise in family life. In short, she wants a wife to share with her all the domestic routines, and then she wants a husband who has the energy and motivation to romance her after doing all the things men usually do, like fixing things and handling emergencies. As men cling to old expectations, women are creating new expectations. These expectations are understandable but unrealistic.

As men cling to old expectations, women are creating
new expectations that are equally unrealistic.

Just as women can't do it all, men can't either. Women today
carry a burden twice that of their mothers. They not only feel the
new economic and social pressure to work outside the home, but
they also experience an ancient genetic pressure to nest. A woman's nurturing instincts and nesting urges produce needs and standards developed by a long lineage of women.

Returning home after work causes
most women's stress levels to increase.

Most men appreciate a beautiful and orderly home, yet they
can easily return to an untended house and simply relax while
watching TV. In his world, relaxing comes before tending to the
home. After a long day at work, a man takes a deep breath and
begins to relax at just the thought of going home. When a woman
returns home, her stress levels go up. Every cell in her body says,
"This house must be cleaned up before we can relax."

Even if she wanted to rest, she couldn't. Her mind is too busy
with standards that she must uphold. This is also true of women
who do not work outside the home. In a woman's mind, there is
a long to-do list. Until it is finished, it is very hard for her to rest,
relax, or do something simply because she enjoys it.

Women are the CEOs of their homes, organizing the household
and determining what has to be accomplished. A woman has to
notice what needs to be done and then enlist her partner's help.

Most husbands will happily do what they are asked to do eventually, but it is rare on Mars to notice that something needs to be done. Sometimes it takes so much nagging to get something accomplished, and when it is done, the task has been performed so halfheartedly that she begins to feel it's easier to do it all herself. Women do not understand why their partners don't feel the same motivation to share the responsibilities of the home, and they resent it.

Under stress, women feel the pressure
of a never-ending to-do list.

Women are the custodians of love, family, and relationship. When women stop being women and are too stressed to carry out these functions, we are all lost. Women remind men of what is important in life. Women hold the wisdom of the heart and inspire men to act from their hearts. Men can have great vision, but women provide the meaningful foundation. When women are not happy, no one is happy.

When women become men, men lose purpose,
meaning, and inspiration in life.

To resolve this source of conflict, men and women need to understand each other better. Men need to recognize what women are going through. A woman already feels enough internal pressure about domestic order. Any extra pressure from him can easily push her over the edge. At the same time, women need to recognize and understand what men can and cannot do to be more supportive.

How to Ask for a Man's Support

Most men are pitching in more with domestic duties when their wives work outside the home to provide for the family. For two-career couples, if the man is not helping out enough, the answer is to ask for his help in very specific ways instead of criticizing and rejecting him. Do not just expect a man to see everything that a woman might think needs to be done, and then to take action. Routine jobs around the house are not urgent in a man's estimation.

One approach that works most of the time is to ask for his help in specific terms. Men love projects. Projects are specific. They have a beginning and an end. He can determine what he is going to do, how he is going to do it, and most important, when he is going to do it. Men will often do what they consider is most important first. When given a project to accomplish, he also senses that his efforts will not be taken for granted. All these ingredients help to give him energy and motivation. Here are some examples of how a woman can ask for a man's support in specific instead of general terms:

If she is tired that night, she can say, "Would you please make dinner tonight, or pick up some takeout?"

If there are piles of laundry, she can say, "Would you help me fold this laundry tonight?"

If she doesn't feel like cleaning up the kitchen, she can say, "Would you do the dishes tonight, please? I need to take a break."

Or if she wants help with the dishes, instead of just expecting him to pitch in, she can simply say, "Would you bring over the plates?" or "Would you wash the pots and pans tonight? I would really appreciate the help."

If she needs something from the grocery store, instead of doing it herself, she could ask, "Would you please drive to the grocery and pick up these items on this list?"

In each of these examples she is giving him a project that has a beginning and an end. Men tend to work best on projects rather than in routines, since routines have no clear beginning or end. When a man is tired, a domestic routine is rarely a priority, as it is for a woman. Even if he is tired, a project with a definite end point or solution will give him extra energy, particularly if a woman's tone of voice or facial expression while making the request indicates that she will appreciate the result of his actions. When he does something to help her rather than because she expects or thinks he should do it, he then feels closer to her and is more willing to help out in the future. This willingness, based on satisfying many of her little requests or projects, actually gives him more energy at home to provide even more support. Eventually, he will get in the habit of helping more and more.

Men tend to work best on projects rather
than in routines.

Realistic Expectations Lead to Real Love

Most men are not equipped to be the domestic/communicative/romantic partners women fantasize about. Although some men attempt to fulfill that fantasy, in the end both partners become frustrated and disappointed. He may try for years, but eventually he runs out of steam. Some men try during the dating stage and then give up, because they can't continue to meet their partner's expectations. When this is the case, a man may suddenly lose interest and not even know why. He is just not that interested in her, not because she is not right for him, but because he is trying to meet unrealistic expectations. Lucky is the woman who is able to appreciate what a man can offer, for she continues to get more and more.

A man loses interest when he senses that
he can't continue to meet a woman's expectations.

Likewise, most women are not equipped to be the domestic/communicative/romantic partners men want. It is unrealistic for a man to expect a woman to create a beautiful home without help and appreciation, always to be in a good mood, never to be needy, and to be romantically available at all times. Many women try to fulfill this fantasy but feel cheated and betrayed when their partners do not return their love.

When men begin to understand a woman's new needs, they are naturally motivated to help out more. Men who make this change must make sure that they take the time they need for themselves as well; otherwise they will both end up overwhelmed and exhausted. Lucky is the man who is able to meet his own needs and then respond to a woman's need for help around the house, good communication, and regular romance, for he comes home to a happy woman.

Fortunately, reality is much more wonderful than fantasy. We seek real love, and if we have the right expectations, we can find it. Together we can make small but significant changes to support each other more effectively. Adjusting, updating, and correcting our expectations can free us from feeling victimized or powerless to get what we need.

In addition, these new insights about our differences help us to recognize and remember the real problem: increasing stress. Instead of blaming our partners, we can blame stress. It is often a mistake to conclude we are too different to make a relationship work. The truth is, stress can drive a wedge between us. By learning how to support ourselves and our partners at times of greater stress, we can learn to lower stress levels. When stress is removed from the formula, our differences are never a problem. When stress is reduced, our differences are a major source of fulfillment.

> When stress is gone,
> our differences are never a problem.

Men and women don't complain about their partners when they are feeling good. Problems and demands emerge when we are under stress. Our unrealistic expectations surface when we attempt to get our partner's help to lower our stress. With a new understanding of how men and women experience and cope with stress differently, we can address the real problem in relationships today.

The problem is never just our partner, but our own inability to cope with stress. When we learn how we can deal with stress more effectively and help our partners cope, the grip of our unrealistic demands is easily released. We are then able to enjoy the feelings of acceptance, trust, and appreciation. It is only then that our relationships can thrive.

> The problem is never just our partner
> but our own inability to cope with stress.

If a man was to yield to the pressure of a woman's unrealistic expectations, he could become a domestic partner, but within a few years all the romance and passion would be gone. When a man becomes more like a woman in a relationship, he will inevitably become overwhelmed, exhausted, and stressed.

To yield to a woman's unrealistic expectations
will eventually exhaust a man.

This role reversal can easily put a damper on romantic feelings. If a man becomes more feminine, the attraction she felt for him in the beginning is lost. Instead of becoming more sensitive, men need to become sensitive to the needs of women. This is what women are really looking for from a man. Certainly a man can be sensitive, but to meet her needs, he must consider her needs and not just his own.

Instead of becoming more sensitive,
men need to become sensitive to the needs of women.

When a man displays a greater sensitivity regarding his own needs and feelings, a woman begins to experience maternal feelings rather than sexual attraction. Instead of feeling cared for, she feels her motherly instinct to care for him. Though this feels loving, it does not promote romantic feelings. On the other hand, when a woman displays sensitivity with appreciation and trust for a man's support, it dramatically increases his sexual interest in her. A woman's sensitivity, which gives her the ability to enjoy and appreciate the little things in life, is a major turn-on to men.

A woman's sensitivity, which gives her the ability
to enjoy and appreciate the little things in life,
is a major turn-on to men.

With new insights about what women need, a man can help a woman cope with stress without increasing his own stress. A man can give the domestic/communicative/romantic support a woman needs, but in ways that work for him as well. Without becoming like a woman, he can provide the support she needs even when it doesn't look the way she thought it should.

A woman can learn ways to lower her partner's stress by helping him feel successful in helping her. Though a man does appreciate domestic support, positive communication, and romance, what is most important to him is to feel he is providing his partner with some measure of fulfillment. Instead of thinking of direct ways to support him, she can actually do less and simply appreciate what he does for her. This works well, because women are already doing way too much. Wouldn't it be great if a woman could do less, and a man would feel more supported? Well, it's true. It is such a new concept for women that it takes a little time to sink in.

When a man takes action to support a woman's needs, she feels supported, and her stress goes down. But the opposite is true on Mars. When a woman does less for him and allows him to do more for her, his stress is lessened. A man's stress is reduced when he feels successful in meeting her needs. Instead of giving more to him, she just needs to help him be successful in meeting her needs.

By giving less, a woman can actually be
more supportive of her partner.

"Helping him help her" as a strategy for success seems very foreign to most women. They don't imagine that they are pushing away his support, but in many ways they are. Every time she complains, every time she makes demands, every time she gets upset, every time she doesn't ask for help, every time she resents having to ask for support, she may be giving him the message that he is not a success. Unknowingly, she is increasing rather than lowering his stress and ultimately pushing his support away.

In short, "helping him help her" involves asking him for support instead of just expecting him to give it, and then requires that she acknowledges how much she authentically appreciates whatever she gets. This is achieved by feeling and being, not by doing. Her "feeling response" to his actions is much more important than anything she can ever directly do for him. By being grateful for what she is getting in her relationship, she is actually helping him to succeed. On the other hand, when a woman focuses on what she is not getting, she gives the message that he is not a success, and his stress goes up. He then has less to give. She is pushing away his love when she focuses on what she is not getting.

> A woman's response to his actions is much more important than anything she can ever directly do for him.

This simple principle can produce immediate results in any relationship. There are endless ways women fail to acknowledge a man's sincere desire to provide his support, just as there are countless ways a man can respond to her needs to provide her with greater fulfillment. Finding authentic ways to give a man the message that his efforts are appreciated does not involve the old-fashioned notion of sacrificing her needs to avoid demanding anything of him. Instead, it requires a greater responsibility to fulfill her own needs and to learn how to ask a man for support in small increments that are realistic and reasonable.

Even when a woman takes time for herself, she can help a man feel like a success in a relationship. When she is happy, he will always take credit and feel better. Without this insight, a woman would never think that taking time for herself could actually help her partner. When men take time for themselves, women often feel neglected. For this reason, a woman might find it hard to believe that taking time for herself actually supports him in giving more to her. Understanding our differences provides a completely new direction for men and women that not only brings out the best in our partners but makes relationships so much easier.

Why Women Need Men

Fully receiving a man's support is not as simple today as it was in the past. Women today are confused when it comes to the role a man can play in their lives. She either needs him to be more like a woman, or she feels she doesn't need him at all. Neither approach works. Being more independent and self-sufficient, modern women want a man to share their lives with but don't really feel the need for a man. They want a man, but to need him makes them cringe. When they do need him, they often want him to be someone he is not and cannot be.

Ultimately, men want to feel needed and are most attracted to a woman who appreciates what they have to offer. When a man is needed, he can make a difference. A woman who can appreciate what a man has to offer automatically reduces the stress in his life. Women who clearly feel the need for a man attract them like bees to honey.

Women who are very successful and independent often remain alone, because they don't realize why they need a man. Statistically, the more financially successful a woman is, the lower her chances of getting married, and the greater the possibility of divorce. Most of these divorces are initiated by the woman. These statistics change as women learn to feel their need for a man and appreciate what he can offer. It is challenging to appreciate someone you do not think you need. When a woman doesn't open herself to a man in this way, she is pushing him away and increasing the stress in his life.

You can only appreciate what you have
when you authentically feel a need for it.

Independent women don't have to give up their freedoms to feel their need for a man. You can be independent about some things and depend on your partner for other things. It doesn't have to be all or nothing. Some women watched their mothers deny their needs and submit themselves to please their husbands. They have vowed never to allow that to happen to them. By seeking a life of complete independence, they, too, are denying their needs and following in their mothers' footsteps. To avoid submitting themselves in a relationship, they have denied their needs altogether.

For other women, the process of surviving or trying to get ahead in their careers distracts them from getting in touch with their feelings and need for a relationship. To get ahead in the workplace, they have to express their more independent selves and have difficulty shifting back to their feminine side that easily feels the need for a man. These women often think they need a more feeling or sensitive man, but they really need to connect with their own more feminine side.

If he is more sensitive, such a woman might imagine that it will be safer for her feminine side to emerge. She has fantasies of talking with her partner the way she would with a girlfriend or with a wise mentor. Unfortunately, when a woman gets a "more feeling man," it doesn't help her connect with her own feelings. The more sensitive a man is, the more their conversations will center on him and not on her. A needy man is a huge turnoff to women. After a while, she doesn't even want to talk with him, because she will have to listen to more of his sensitive feelings or his opinionated tirades. When she thinks she needs a more sensitive and vulnerable man, what she really needs is to express her more vulnerable self. What she really needs is to be heard, which all men can learn to do.

A needy man is a huge turnoff to women.

Other women, who are able to feel their needs but don't understand how men are different, expect them to react and respond the way a woman would. For these women, determining what they need in a relationship and what is possible can be very confusing. The days of women needing a man just for survival and security are gone.

So what do modern women need? When I ask this question, single women often have no idea. At first, they don't even want to admit that they need a man. They prefer to have a partner. They want to share their lives with someone, but they don't need a man. Needing a man would make these women feel weak rather than just feminine.

Women need to rediscover the power and strength of their femininity. Women don't have to be like men to be powerful and get what they want and need. Likewise, men don't have to become like women to be loving and supportive in their relationships.

Many successful women are repelled
by the idea that they might need a man.

Needing a partner is not a weakness. It is why we partner up.
Men and women just have different primary needs. Men need to
feel needed, and women need to feel they are not alone. Just as a
woman is happiest when she feels she is getting what she needs
from her partner, a man is happiest when he feels successful in
meeting his partner's needs. This is an important distinction. We
certainly need each other, but for different reasons.

Men need to feel needed,
and women need to feel they are not alone.

Feeling that he makes a difference reduces a man's stress. It is
what gives men a reason for living. On the other hand, feeling that
she is not alone and that she can get what she needs reduces a
woman's stress. When a women feels she can open up and depend
on someone, her stress in life is greatly reduced. When a woman
is unable to recognize her needs or get them met, she increasingly
feels distress in her life, and then wonders why she doesn't sleep
well at night.

Independent and successful women often ask me why their husbands are so tired. With this new insight, it becomes clear. If she is
unaware of her need for him, then he is not empowered by her love
and appreciation. Instead, he becomes exhausted in her presence.

When a woman learns to feel her feminine side and identify
her true needs for a man, her appreciation can bring out the best in

her partner. Rather than becoming tired when he interacts with her, he is energized.

Many women today are under so much stress that they are simply unable to feel their needs. Under stress, women tend to reach out and feel the needs of others rather than their own. With a little time and exploration, these strong and independent women discover and admit to a variety of needs, most commonly:

- She needs a man for romantic companionship.
- She needs a man to be faithful.
- She needs a man for simple companionship. She doesn't want to come home to a big, beautiful, empty house or apartment.
- She needs a man for financial backup—someone who could support her if she couldn't work.
- She needs a man around because she feels safer—two people are twice as good as one.
- She needs to have a partner to share fun times with.
- She needs a partner to share with who cares about her well-being.
- She needs a partner who misses her when he is away.
- She needs a partner to help raise the family if they have children.
- She needs a partner if she doesn't want to have children alone.
- She needs a partner to have a family.
- She needs a partner to share the responsibilities of caring for the nest.
- She needs a partner to fix things when they break. She doesn't want to do her own plumbing anymore.
- She needs a partner's support to feel really great.

The truth is, women today need men more than ever. They just need men in different ways. Men can provide special support that can assist women in coping with the new stresses of modern life, but most women don't know how to get this support or to appreciate it properly when it is available. With a greater awareness of her needs, a woman can begin to appreciate what she is getting and focus less on what she is not getting. With a more realistic vision of what is possible rather than the Hollywood fantasy of a man who fulfills her every wish, she is better able to appreciate his efforts and not take for granted all the things her partner already does provide.

When she learns to appreciate what a man already offers, a woman holds the key to asking for more in small reasonable increments to get the support she needs and deserves. This is not only a formula for success, but it is also what real love is all about.

I remember when this idea became very clear to me about six years into my own marriage with my wife, Bonnie. After some particularly great lovemaking, I commented, "This was as good as it was in the beginning."

Her response taught me something important. She said that making love that night was actually better than in the beginning, because, as she explained, "In the beginning, we didn't really know each other. Now you have seen the best of me and the worst of me, and you still adore me. That is real love."

Bonnie helped me to have a richer understanding of lasting love. Love is not a fantasy of perfection in which our every need is met, but sharing a life together, striving to meet each other's needs as best we can. Forgiving our partners for their mistakes and accepting their limitations can be just as fulfilling as appreciating their many gifts and successes. Just as it was difficult for her to live with a man who didn't always measure up to her expectations, it was challenging for me to accept that I could not and did not provide everything her fantasy of a perfect relationship included.

Just as women need to let go of expecting men to be perfect, men need to let go of expecting women to think we are perfect. Together we have learned that our life does not have to be perfect for us to connect and support each other. Real love does not demand perfection but actually embraces imperfection. Sharing this kind of love enriches all aspects of our lives and brings increasing fulfillment.

Real love does not demand perfection
but actually embraces imperfection.

Intimate and truly loving relationships make up the fabric of a fulfilling life. The relentless demands in our lives to have more, go faster, and do better can distract us from this simple truth. The social changes that have expanded our freedoms have also created the need for new ways to keep harmony in our most intimate relationships. In the pages that follow, you will gain new insight, allowing you and your partner to come together in harmony, ease, love, and mutual fulfillment.

CHAPTER TWO

HARDWIRED TO BE DIFFERENT

The first step in understanding and accepting our differences is to recognize that men and women are actually hardwired to be different. The way our brains are structured and function is not the same. Although some of our differences result from parental or social conditioning, we will explore how and why we are biologically different.

Acknowledging these hardwired gender differences helps us to identify and release our unrealistic expectations that our partners be more like us and to accept that we are not the same. At first, these differences may seem to be a hindrance, but once you fully understand the biology, it becomes clear that we complement each other perfectly. In fact, it is as if men and women were made for each other.

If we cannot find a way to embrace the differences and to achieve a balance, sustaining a relationship is difficult. Many couples never develop their relationships beyond dating. Others make a commitment, but over time, their differences erode their intimacy, and they split up. In these instances, both believe that there was not enough common ground to make a relationship work. Though some-times couples are not compatible, usually their problems derive from not understanding their differences. Here are some expressions of how we feel when we don't understand our differences:

SHE SAYS:	HE SAYS:
"He was just too stubborn to change."	"She used to appreciate everything I did, but gradually she wanted to change me."
"He was so self-centered. He wasn't even interested in my life or my feelings."	"She was too needy. Everything was about her."
"He became so cold and detached. I didn't feel safe to open up with him."	"Everything was about her feelings. I felt completely controlled."
"I used to be number one, but as soon as he got me, work became his number-one priority."	"Gradually, the kids became more important than me."
"He never listens to what I say. All he wants to do is solve my problems."	"She gets so emotional and then makes no sense at all."
"He was afraid of intimacy. Every time we would get closer, he would pull away."	"She was so responsive in the beginning. Now I feel like I have to fill out a form before we have sex."
"Everything started out fine, and then he changed."	"She was too high-maintenance. Whatever I did, it was never enough. There was always something I did wrong."

If you have read my previous books, you know that the root cause of these complaints is a lack of understanding and acceptance of our basic differences. They are certainly legitimate complaints, but they emerge because we fail to take our differences into account.

If you have ever said, felt, or heard your partner utter one of the criticisms listed above, your resistance to natural differences may be at the root of many of your collisions. When you resist rather than support your partner's needs when he or she is coping with stress, you will evoke the worst of your partner's character. If you are single, this insight might make you aware that you have alienated a potential partner or that your behavior may have been misinterpreted by another. Whether you are married or single, a new understanding and acceptance of how we are supposed to be different will enable you to bring out the best in your partner and yourself as well.

Married couples with good relationships often report that they have stopped trying to change each other. But acceptance of our differences does not mean accepting any behavior, however negative. Instead, loving acceptance provides a foundation from which we can work with our differences, so that both partners get what they need most. Accepting our differences is not always easy, especially when we are under stress, but the advice in these pages can help to smooth the way.

Radically Different Responses to Stress

The responses to stress are very different on Mars and Venus. Men tend to shift gears, disengage, and forget their problems, while women are compelled to connect, ask questions, and share problems. This simple distinction can be extremely destructive in a relationship if it is not appreciated and respected.

When a man needs time alone or doesn't want to talk about his day, it doesn't mean that he cares less for his partner. When a woman wants to talk about her day, it doesn't mean she is excessively needy or high-maintenance. His detached manner doesn't mean he doesn't care, and her stronger emotional reactions do not mean she doesn't appreciate all that he does to provide for her.

If a man forgets a woman's need or a woman
remembers his mistakes, it doesn't mean
they don't love each other.

By understanding our differences, we can correctly interpret our partners' behavior and feelings and give our partners what they need most, which will inevitably bring out their best side. Instead of seeing our different stress reactions as a problem, we need to recognize that our attempts to change our partners are most often the real problem.

Instead of seeing our different stress reactions
as a problem, we need to recognize
that our attempts to change our partners
are most often the real problem.

Understanding the biological reasons for the different ways we perceive and behave in the world enables us to be realistic about what to expect from our partners.

Skills Are Different on Mars and Venus

As you have already noticed in daily life, men and women behave, think, feel, and react in dissimilar ways. It is obvious that men and women do not process language, emotion, and information in the same way. But now we have a way to make sense of this difference. Although happily married couples have already figured this out, finally the academic and scientific community has verified our different gender-related tendencies.

Edward O. Wilson, a world-famous sociobiologist from Harvard University, has systematically observed our gender tendencies. He found that women are more empathetic and security-seeking than men and have more developed verbal and social skills. In comparison, men tend to be more independent, aggressive, and dominant and demonstrate greater spatial and mathematical skills.

In practical terms, this means that situations that could be simple to resolve become very tedious and tiresome when we don't understand and accept our differences. For example, when you discuss how you are going to invest your savings, a man is generally more of a risk taker and a woman will be more conservative. Certainly how we are raised will make a big difference, but generally speaking, men feel more comfortable taking risks, while women prioritize security. With an understanding of this difference, a man doesn't have to take it personally when she asks more questions. She is not necessarily mistrusting him but simply seeking to meet her greater need for security. When he is more impulsive and wants to find solutions right away, she can realize this is his nature rather than misinterpret his tone by presuming he doesn't care about what she feels, wants, or needs.

Studies confirm there are real differences in the way men and women estimate time, judge speed, do math, orient themselves in space, and visualize objects in 3-D. Men tend to excel in these skills. Women have more developed relationship abilities, sensitivity to emotions in others, emotional and aesthetic expression and appreciation, and language skills. Women are adept at performing detailed, planned tasks.

Without an understanding of this last difference, a woman can feel neglected when a man waits to the last minute to plan time with her or when he doesn't anticipate her needs. If a woman understands these differences, she no longer resents needing to ask for support, because she realizes that his brain simply doesn't work the way hers does. In the event that her partner does something without her having to ask, she will appreciate the extra effort he is making rather than taking it for granted.

Women's brains are designed to consider and anticipate the emotions, sensitivities, and needs of others. Men, on the other hand, are more acutely aware of their own needs, or at least their needs for achieving the goal at hand. Since men were hunters for thousands of years, they needed this ability to protect themselves in the wild. In the home camp, a woman's life insurance was making sure she cared for others. If she did so, then they would care for her at her time of need.

When you write your will, you have the opportunity to donate your body organs to help others after you die. Faced with this option, nine out of ten women donate their organs, while nine out of ten men do not. By nature, women tend to be giving, even after their death. A woman's greatest challenge in learning to cope more effectively with stress is to begin caring for herself as much as she is caring for others.

A woman's greatest challenge is to begin caring for herself as much as she is caring for others.

Why Our Brains Developed Differently

Our brains might have developed the way they did because cavemen and cavewomen had very defined roles to ensure their survival. Our male ancestors hunted and needed to travel long distances in pursuit of game. Strong navigational skills allowed men to become better hunters and providers. A man had to depend on himself to find his way home. In those days, asking for directions was not always an option.

Our female ancestors gathered food near the home and cared for the children. They formed strong emotional attachments to their children and the other women, on whom they depended when the men were hunting. Women had to track their immediate environment as they gathered nuts and berries for survival. Maybe that's why women today have the ability to find things around the home and in the refrigerator that their partners seem to be incapable of seeing.

Scientists speculate that women's advantage in verbal skills could have resulted from their physical size. Men had the bodily strength to fight with other men. Women used language instead to argue and persuade. Women also used language because they could. When a man was in danger, he needed to stay quiet much of the time. To this day, faced with stress, a man will often become quiet. As a result, men go to their cave to recover from stress, while women have adapted by learning to talk about their stresses. By letting others know about her problems, she would make it easier to get their support. Unless she talked, others simply would not know what she needed.

Our brains developed with gender differences to ensure our survival. These adaptations have taken thousands of years to occur. It is unrealistic to expect our brains to change suddenly to adapt to the vast changes in our gender roles in the last fifty years. These changes are at the core of the stress that is causing Mars and Venus to collide. If we are to thrive and not just survive, we need to update our relationship skills in ways that reflect our natural abilities, tendencies, and needs.

The advances in neuroscientific research have allowed scientists to discover significant anatomical and neuropsychological differences between male and female brains that explain our observable behavioral differences.

Single Focus on Mars / Multitasking on Venus

A woman's brain has a larger corpus callosum, the bundle of nerves that connects the right and left hemispheres of the brain. This link, which produces cross-talk between the hemispheres, is 25 percent smaller in men. In practical terms, this means men do not connect feelings and thoughts as readily as women do. In a very real sense, women have superhighways connecting their feelings to speech, while men have back roads with plenty of stop signs. Some researchers believe that the integration of the two lobes may be the source of "women's intuition"—in other words, whole-brain processing.

This stronger connection between different parts of the brain increases a woman's ability to multitask. When she is listening, she is also thinking, remembering, feeling, and planning all at the same time.

A man's brain is single-focused,
while a woman's brain tends to multitask.

A man's brain is highly specialized, using a specific part of a single hemisphere to accomplish a task. A woman's brain is more diffuse, using both hemispheres for many tasks. This neurological difference allows men to focus and to block out distractions for long periods of time. On the other hand, women tend to see things in a broader context, from a larger vantage point.

Men tend to do one thing at a time in their brains and in life. When a man is under stress, he can easily forget his partner and her needs. He may be focusing on how to get that promotion, so he forgets to bring home the milk. A woman can easily misinterpret his forgetful behavior as uncaring. After she has misunderstood his behavior in this manner, it is even harder for her to risk asking him for more support.

This insight can help a woman not to take it personally when he is at his computer and seems annoyed when she asks him a question. For her, it is a simple task to shift her attention when she is interrupted, but for him it is much more difficult. If he seems annoyed, she can remember that it is much more difficult for him to shift gears rather than take it personally.

In a similar manner, women become annoyed when a man tries to narrow down the focus of her conversation to a single point. He may interrupt her and ask her to get to the point, or ask what she wants him to do when she is still just connecting all the dots of what she is talking about. Quite commonly men will say, "I understand," but a woman hears that he wants her to finish talking.

He feels she doesn't have to continue, because he understands. Since she is still in the process of discovering what it is she wants to say, she knows he cannot fully understand. There is not just one point when she is expressing herself. By taking more time to listen to her many details, a man helps his partner to come back to a more centered and stress-free perspective.

Likewise, when a woman minimizes her interruptions of a man's focused activities, she helps him to keep his stress levels down. Leaving a man alone and ignoring him is sometimes the best way to support him. Understanding that these tendencies are based on our brain differences frees us from taking things personally and reveals practical ways to support our partners in coping better with their stresses.

Leaving a man alone and ignoring him
is sometimes the best way to support him.

Men separate information, emotions, and perceptions into separate compartments in their brains, while women tend to link their experiences together, reacting to multiple issues with their whole brain. This is one of the reasons a woman has a greater tendency to become overwhelmed with too much to do when she is under stress. While women tend to reach out to take in more information, under stress men tend to focus on the most important thing to do.

While women tend to reach out to take in more
information, under stress men tend to focus on
determining the most important thing to do.

This difference in brain structure between men and women has another important effect on stress relief. A man can more easily disengage from his serious, responsible left brain and allow it to rest and regenerate. When a man is stressed, he can simply change his focus to a hobby or watching TV and he begins to relax. He shifts from using his left brain, which is logical, practical, and reality-based, to his right brain, which is feeling, risk-taking, and fantasy-based. By making this shift, he automatically disconnects from the stress of his responsibilities. In this manner, a man can shift gears and disengage from everyday worries with greater ease.

A woman does not have this luxury, since the connective tissue between the two hemispheres of her brain won't allow her to disengage as easily. When she is on the right side of her brain, trying to relax or have a fun time, she is still connected to her analytical and rational left brain.

On a practical note, understanding this difference helps men to recognize the futility of making comments to a woman like "Just forget it" or "Don't worry about it." She can't make this shift the way a man does, but she can talk about what is bothering her. On Mars, if a man can't solve a problem, his way of coping is to forget about it until he can do something about it. On Venus, if a woman can't solve a problem, then she feels, "At least we can talk about it." Talking with someone who cares about her well-being has the power to stimulate the neurotransmitters needed to reduce stress levels in a woman's brain. By remembering her problems, a woman can actually free herself from their gripping hold on her and her mood.

White Matter vs. Gray Matter

Men and women possess two different types of brains, designed equally for intelligent behavior. Men have approximately 6.5 times as much gray matter as women. Women have almost 10 times the white matter that men do. Information-processing centers are located in gray matter. The connections or networks among these processing centers are composed of white matter. These differences explain why men tend to excel in tasks involving gray matter local processing—like mathematics—while women excel at integrating and assimilating information from gray matter regions, required for language skills, because of their abundance of connecting white matter.

This physical difference in our brain composition helps explain why we communicate so differently. A woman's brain is busy connecting everything. The more she cares about something, the more she connects it to other things going on in her brain.

For example, when she sees a movie or visits a friend, she may have a lot to say about it. Meanwhile a guy may have nothing to say unless the movie happens to hit a particular area of interest. She assumes that he does not want to talk about the movie, but he actually has little to say. With this new insight, she can be assured that he is interested in hearing what she has to say, even though he has little to offer in return. When a woman gives up expecting her partner to talk more, not only does he appreciate her willingness to talk, but gradually he begins to share more.

When men have little to say, women often take it
personally, as if he doesn't want to share.

This same idea applies to asking a man about his day or a trip he has taken. When he has little to say, he is not intentionally hiding what happened; he just doesn't think that much about it, and as a consequence he doesn't remember much. She looks forward to explaining how everything connects. The process of communicating actually helps her brain reduce stress levels, while it has little benefit for him.

Why Talk Is Big on Venus

Two sections of the brain, Broca's area in the frontal lobe and Wernicke's area in the temporal lobe, are associated with language. These areas are larger in women, and that explains why women are so verbal. Researchers have located six or seven language centers in both hemispheres of a woman's brain, but for men, language is only located in the left hemisphere. Since men have fewer language centers, it is not only harder for them to express what they experience, but they do not feel the need.

A man's language centers are particularly activated when he is solving a problem. Some men will talk more at the beginning of the relationship, because at that time a man is primarily introducing himself, and talking is a way to "solve the problem" of letting her know about himself and how he feels for her. Once that problem is solved, his language centers are not easily activated. Likewise, his listening center is most active when he is solving a problem.

Women's brains are constructed to communicate and express feelings. Compared to a man's brain, a woman's is much busier, always articulating reactions and perceptions. Many parts of her brain are fully engaged when she is talking. Men have a harder time connecting their emotions with their thoughts and articulating what they feel. This difference is a source of much friction in relationships. Understanding that a man is not withholding when he is silent can release a woman from the frustration of getting her partner to talk about his day in greater detail.

With practice, a man can learn to be a good listener, which is actually one of the most potent ways to help a woman lower her stress levels. A woman may like it when a man opens up and shares, but unless she first feels heard, it will not lower her stress. As men get better at listening to women and women get better at appreciating this step, men become more open and share more.

Math vs. Feelings

The IPL (inferior parietal lobule) is a region on both sides of the brain, located just above the level of the ears. The size of the IPL correlates with mathematical ability. An enlarged left IPL was found in Albert Einstein's brain, as well as in those of other physicists and mathematicians. The left IPL, more developed in men, is involved with perception of time and speed and the ability to rotate 3-D figures. These abilities have a lot to do with the Martian love of video games. More than 90 percent of video game users are from Mars.

This is also why men seem to rush women to the point when they are talking or making decisions. He is acutely aware of the time she is taking to talk. While listening, he is also working hard to determine what needs to be done to solve her problem as soon as possible. This is not because he doesn't care about her, but because he does. He wants to help, but doesn't realize it would be an even greater help to ask more questions rather than rush to the point.

When women talk, a man is acutely aware of the time
she is taking and feels an inner urgency to help
her solve her problems.

In women, the right side of the IPL is larger. The left side of the brain has more to do with more linear, reasonable, and rational thought, while the right side of the brain is more emotional, feeling, and intuitive. Men are typically drawn to solving problems, while women have the tendency to understand the dynamics of a problem, the various relationships between the different parts of a problem.

Women can also become frustrated when someone is taking too long to get to the point. By multiplying this frustration by ten, you have what the average man experiences listening to his wife complain about a list of problems in her life. This does not mean that she cannot share her feelings, but it does mean she has to do so in a manner that will work for him as well. We will explore this art in chapter 9.

The IPL also allows the brain to process information from the senses, particularly in selective attention, like when women are able to respond to a baby's crying in the night.

Studies have shown that the right LPL, dominant in women, is linked to the memory and manipulation of spatial relationships. It is also related to the perception of our own feelings—a driving force on Venus.

While men are particularly good at following the ball on a football field at a distance, women are adept at noticing subtleties of their own feelings and others'. One of the problems women have is accurately interpreting a man's feelings. For example, he looks frustrated, and she thinks he is not interested in what she is saying. In truth, he is simply trying to make sense of what she is saying so that he can be of help. She is correct in noticing his frustration, but her interpretation can be completely off the mark.

Our Brains Differ in Response to Danger

The amygdala, an almond-shaped structure found toward the front on both sides of the brain just beneath the surface, determines our brain's response to danger. The amygdala operates differently in men and women. The right side is more active in men, with more connections to other areas of the brain, while the left side is more active in women. In a man's brain, there are more connections from the amygdala to the visual cortex, which means men are more reactive to visual stimuli than women.

This explains why men have a greater tendency to stare at other women. Men's brains are just more active in this way. When a man is presented with a challenge—and women are definitely a challenge to men—his visual cortex becomes activated. His instinct to look at other women is not a sign he doesn't love his partner, but a manifestation of what stimulates energy in his brain. This important insight is not an excuse for insensitive behavior. When a man looks at another woman, he should also be respectful of his partner and make it brief, and then show a little more attention or affection to his partner. If I look too long, my wife just gives me a friendly elbow jab to my side. Once she said, "It's okay to look, just don't drool!"

Looking at women is a healthy instinct in men.

This kind of attitude gives the right message to a man. It is accepting but also asks him to consider that it could embarrass her if her husband is staring too long at another woman. On one hand, she asks for what she would like, and on the other hand, she doesn't reject or shame him for this tendency. It is a good thing he is attracted to women. That is why he is attracted to his wife. Just because he responds visually to other women, that doesn't mean he is not attracted to or in love with his wife. If he doesn't feel safe being attracted to women in her presence, his attraction to her will lessen as well.

In addition, the amygdala in a man's brain is directly connected to the action center of the brain. This tends to make men more impatient or impulsive when there are urgent problems to be solved.

The amygdala, which in part determines our reactions
to stress and danger, is directly wired to the visual
and take-action part of a man's brain.

In a woman's brain, the more active left amygdala is connected to other regions of the brain, including the hypothalamus, which receives signals from sensors in the body, rather than external stimulation. A woman's amygdala is directly linked to regions of her brain that are associated with feeling rather than action. The left-hemisphere connection in women controls the environment within the body, which adds to a woman's sensitivity to what is going on inside her. Some researchers believe this difference developed because the female body had to deal with internal stressors like pregnancy and childbirth. In a man's brain, the areas that connect with the amygdala react to the external environment.

This physiological difference helps us to understand why men become impatient when women talk about a problem, and want to do something about it. His amygdala, which is about twice as big as hers, is directly linked to a visual and action part of the brain that is "looking for a solution," or something to do. Unlike a man, a woman's amygdala is directly linked to other parts of her brain that are more feeling-oriented than action-oriented. While he wants to do something, she will want to explore her feelings about the problem.

Why Women Never Forget a Quarrel

Women's brains are wired to feel and recall emotions more intensely than the brains of men. The process of experiencing emotion and coding that experience into memory is more tightly integrated in a woman's brain, and her neural responses are more tightly integrated. Though scientists have not yet been able to identify the neural basis for the difference, studies have found that women tend to have more vivid and stronger memories of emotional events than men. Compared to men, women can recall more memories more quickly. Their memories are richer and more intense.

When under stress, a woman's mind can become flooded with these memories.

Emotions enhance a woman's memory.

There is a physical explanation for why women are able to call up slights, wrongs, and fights from the past. The amygdala does play a key role in emotional responses and emotional memory. In the past, the amygdala was believed to be involved primarily with fear and other negative emotions. Recent studies have shown that the amygdala responds to the strength or intensity of both pleasant and unpleasant stimulation. Neural connections from this structure to the rest of the brain enable it to respond quickly to sensory input and influence psychological and behavioral responses.

Forming an emotional memory occurs in the left amygdala in women, and the right amygdala in men. In women, the brain regions involved in emotional reactions coincide with the regions that encode the memory of an experience. These processes occur in different hemispheres for men. Researchers suggest that the neural connections between the emotional and memory centers in women might explain why a woman's emotional memory is more vivid and accurate than a man's. Just as a woman can remember negative emotions, when stress levels drop, she has a much greater capacity to remember all the good things a man has done. It is this trait that can make women so attractive to men. While he easily forgets his greatness, her loving responses remind him that he does make a difference.

Women who expect men to express the same degree of intensity and accuracy as they do when it comes to relationships will be disappointed. Once she recognizes this distinction, a woman can easily adjust her expectations. She is not "lowering her expecta-tions"; she is simply adjusting them to what is realistic. For example, a woman might vividly remember and treasure a particularly roman-tic moment and become deflated when her partner has no recollec-tion of an exchange that had become so important to her. Rather than feeling hurt or angry, she should understand that our brains are wired differently. As I have already pointed out, accepting reality, even though it doesn't measure up to a Hollywood romantic script, enables us to know and experience the rich fulfillment of real love, a love that does not demand perfection in ourselves or our partners.

Depth of Feeling

The limbic system, which includes the hypothalamus, hippocampus, and amygdala, is the seat of emotion and motivation. A woman has a larger, deeper limbic system, which makes her more in touch with her feelings. A woman's increased ability to bond and feel connected to others lies in this part of her brain. Researchers suggest the greater development of this part of the brain leaves women more susceptible to depression. On the other hand, when properly stimulated through loving support and nourished by healthy nutrients, a woman's brain is capable of feeling a much greater degree of fulfillment than men. It is for this reason that men are so drawn to women. A woman's enor-mous capacity for joy, delight, and fulfillment is the fuel that lets a man know that he makes a difference. By nurturing his spirit in this way, she also can find a greater peace deep in her soul.

A woman's enormous capacity for joy, delight,
and fulfillment is the fuel that lets a man know
that he makes a difference.

If we are to thrive and not just survive, we need to update our relationship skills in ways that reflect our natural abilities, tendencies, and needs.

Creating Harmony

This quick survey of our brain differences should convince you that expecting women to be like men and men to be like women is counterproductive. Understanding these fundamental distinctions in our hardwiring should assist us to interpret the behavior of our partners in a more positive light and free us from unrealistic expectations that they think, feel, and act the way we do.

By understanding our differences, we can begin today applying new insights and strategies to support each other in lowering stress levels. The most effective way to do this is to respect our differences—which are anatomical and hardwired in our brains. Instead of clashing to try to get more from our partners, we can focus on creating harmony by giving ourselves what we need so that we have more to give our partners.

By focusing on giving ourselves what we need,
we will have more to give our partners.

Just as the planets do not collide when they assume their natural course around the sun, men and women do not have to clash. The conflict is over when we discover that even our brains are designed to balance each other. A woman wants to be happy, and her man wants to make her so. When she is happy, they are both happy.

In the next chapter, we will examine the significant hormonal differences between men and women and how stress throws our chemistry out of balance. The result is that on Mars, stress stimulates the fight-or-flight response, and on Venus, the response is to tend and befriend.

CHAPTER THREE

STRESS HORMONES
FROM MARS AND VENUS

Being in love stimulates a cascade of hormones that temporarily lowers stress levels. Hormones are chemical messengers that act as a catalyst for chemical changes at the cellular level that affect growth, development, energy, and mood. When we are in love, we feel on top of the world. We are filled with energy. We are euphoric. We are ardent about our new love, and consequently we are more generous in accepting or overlooking our differences. In the early stage of love, we are eager to support our partners' needs. Taking care of his partner boosts special hormones in a man, while being provided for stimulates different hormones in a woman. When these hormones are abundant at the start of a relationship, the stress, clamor, and pressure of our daily lives dissolves into the background.

Once the newness of love wears off, familiarity and routine set in. Feel-good hormone levels begin to drop, and stress levels begin to rise. It is as if love gives us about three years of blissful hormones for free, but after the honeymoon period is over, we have to earn them. We have to manage our own stress levels as we interact with each other.

Adrenaline and Cortisol—
The Red-Alert Hormones

When we think about stress, we think about traffic jams, unpaid bills, messy homes, tension in the workplace, too much to do, deadlines, no one to turn to, crying children—the list is endless. These are certainly some of our daily causes of stress, but not what researchers refer to when they measure our bodies' stress levels. The production of adrenaline and cortisol, hormones secreted by the adrenal gland, is how our bodies respond to outside stress. On a very physical level, these stress hormones can gradually deplete our supply of feel good hormones.

If we are in danger—let's say, chased by a bear—the adrenal gland releases adrenaline (also known as epinephrine), cortisol, and other hormones to give us a temporary burst of energy and mental clarity. For our ancient ancestors, these hormones were a survival mechanism in dangerous situations. Either we escaped, or we were eaten. When adrenaline and cortisol are released, extra energy is directed to the brain and muscles, sharpening our senses and increasing our strength and stamina. This sudden focus redirects energy temporarily from other systems, slowing digestion and other secondary functions. When a bear is chasing you, your body automatically protects itself from being digested rather than digesting lunch.

Adrenaline and cortisol serve an important survival function in life-and-death situations, but the body is not designed to accommodate the continual release of stress hormones. When we are under unrelenting but not life-threatening stress, these hormones are still released, and over time they disrupt our digestive and immune systems, resulting in lower energy and susceptibility to illness. With long-term stress, cortisol and adrenaline create unhealthy fluctuations in our blood sugar levels that can produce moodiness, mild depression, a sense of urgency, irritability, anxiety, and general distress. And all these can affect our relationships. These are some common examples of how stress affects us and thus our relationships:

1. Mild depression inhibits our passion.
2. A sense of urgency takes away our patience and flexibility.
3. A sense of distress, anxiety, or panic greatly diminishes our capacity to be happy.
4. Irritability overshadows our feelings of affection, appreciation, and tenderness.
5. Decreased energy limits how much we can freely give of ourselves.
6. With unstable blood sugar levels, our moods either become flat or fluctuate too much.
7. Men lose interest in the relationship, while women feel overwhelmed, with too much to do and not enough time or support.

When we understand the common symptoms of chronic stress, we can recognize why so many relationships fail today. Learning how stress affects our day-to-day behavior should motivate us to lower our own stress levels. By updating our relationship skills, we can convert our relationships to lower stress levels rather than being another source of stress.

Another Costly Side Effect of Elevated Stress Hormones

Scientists have found a link between cortisol and obesity and increased fat storage in the body. Stress and elevated cortisol levels tend to cause fat to deposit in the abdominal area, which is considered toxic fat, because it leads to strokes and heart attacks.

High cortisol levels can also lead to poor eating habits. While studying eating disorders, some researches discovered that women with stress-induced high levels of cortisol were more likely to snack on high-fat or highly refined carbohydrate foods than women who did not secrete as much cortisol. This new research provides a useful insight into how stress can affect food cravings that lead to unhealthy eating. Have you ever noticed that when you are tired or stressed, you reach for some processed carbohydrate like cookies, chips, or soda? This is because under stress the body gets its energy from carbohydrates.

Cortisol simulates insulin release, which results in an increase in appetite. This terrible cycle will cause you to gain weight and can eventually lead to diabetes and a host of other diseases. The effects of high cortisol levels make it clear how important a healthy diet is when you are under stress. You might feel you do not have time to eat and prepare healthy meals, but maintaining good eating habits is even more important when you and your family are rushing through your lives. One of the ways you can know what foods are not good for you is simply to observe what foods you crave when you are under stress. These are the very foods that will eventually make you feel even worse and put on extra weight.

And let's face it, not only do we feel better when we are at a healthy weight, but we feel more attractive without the excess pounds. When you are feeling attractive, your partner becomes more attracted to you.

We have to learn to manage our stress so that we can grow old together both in love and good health. Heart disease, cancer, diabetes, and obesity have all been directly linked to chronically high levels of cortisol. If we learn to lower our stress levels, we will not only be healthier but will awaken our potential for increased energy, passion, patience, and happiness.

One of the big differences between men and women is that under stress, women produce much more cortisol than men. This helps explain why women have more challenges with weight gain. When cortisol is elevated, we only burn carbohydrates or sugars for energy rather than a healthy combination of carbohydrate and fat. When you cannot burn fat efficiently, it is not only more difficult to lose weight, but you have less energy. Burning fat gives you twenty times more energy than burning carbohydrate. Think of it this way: burning fat gives us the lasting energy of burning logs, but carbohydrates only give us the quick, temporary energy of kindling.

There is another costly effect of high cortisol levels on a woman's body. The by-product of burning carbohydrates is lactic acid. If a woman's body is burning carbohydrates instead of fat, her levels of lactic acid rise. With excess lactic acid buildup, calcium is leached from the bones to neutralize these acids. This helps explain why 80 percent of the people who have osteoporosis are women.

Billions of dollars each year are spent on antidepressants to assist men and women to cope with stress. Fortunately there are natural ways to reduce stress levels that do not have the dangerous side effects of taking medications. I have spent the last ten years researching this subject, and present a variety of ways for both women and men to cope with anxiety and depression using cleansing food plans, healthy fats, and natural supplements. More about this can be found at my Web site, www.marsvenuswellness.com, or in my last book, *The Mars and Venus Diet and Exercise Solution.*

Hormones Are from Heaven

At the start of a relationship, a man will get excited and motivated by the challenge of winning a woman's affection. The challenge automatically stimulates the production of testosterone, the hormone from Mars that contributes to a man's sense of power and well-being. When his testosterone levels are at normal levels, he is pumped and is more attentive and attracted to his partner.

As routine sets in over time, and the challenge in the relationship decreases, his testosterone levels decrease. When this happens, the honeymoon is over, and a man looks to stimulate higher levels of testosterone. Work outside the home will almost always provide new challenges to capture a man's interest and raise his testosterone levels. A man's loss of passion occurs on a biological level as he shifts from being enraptured by a relationship to refocusing on work.

Similarly, when a woman gets to know her partner and feels safe with him, there is an increase in the production of oxytocin, known as the cuddle hormone. Just as a man responds to the levels of testosterone in his body, a woman experiences more energy, happiness, flexibility, and attraction for her partner when her oxytocin levels rise.

Over time, as reality sets in and her expectations are not always satisfied, she no longer assumes that all her needs will be met. The resulting decrease in hope, trust, and optimism will affect her oxytocin levels. Her daily routine loses some of its magic. She attempts to bring back the magic by giving more to their relationship, but when her attempts are not reciprocated, she eventually loses the glow, along with the motivation to give more. His detachment and her increased attention to their lack of connection will inevitably build tension in the relationship. A closer look at testosterone and oxytocin will explain how men and women respond differently to stress, and what you can do to accommodate those differences and achieve harmony.

The King of Hormones

Testosterone, the principle male sex hormone, is one of the key elements in determining sexual characteristics in men, including dominance, emotional and physical strength, body shape, hairiness, deep voice, odor, and sexual performance. The hormone also plays a role in assertiveness and drive, competitiveness, creativity, intellect, and the ability to frame and execute new ideas. Women produce it too, but adult males produce twenty to thirty times more testosterone than do women.

Adult males produce twenty to thirty times
more testosterone than do women.

Testosterone affects general health throughout life and helps to develop strong muscles and bones. Having the right level of testosterone helps men cope with stress. The right level is what matters—not too high nor too low. Testosterone can increase significantly with acute stress and may cause increased aggressiveness. Researchers have found that stress is chronic in so many of our lives today. This causes testosterone levels to plunge. A drop in testosterone has been associated with irritable male syndrome, characterized by withdrawal, irritability, and depression. A new study has found that levels of testosterone of men in the United States have been falling steadily during the past twenty years.

Researchers have found that testosterone levels have
fallen in American men during the last twenty years.

Factors like aging, smoking, and obesity do not fully explain the decline. A diet high in meat and poultry might contribute to the downward trend, because the hormones used in meat production act like estrogen in the body. Estrogen, the female sex hormone, inhibits the production of testosterone. Alcohol and soy products also have a negative effect on testosterone levels. Beer, for example, contains plant estrogens that can eventually reduce testosterone levels, one of the reasons intoxication and sex sometimes do not mix.

Achieving, Appreciation, and Success

Normal levels of testosterone are linked to feelings of success in men. To feel good in a relationship, a man needs to feel successful at providing for his partner's fulfillment. Her responses of trust, acceptance, and appreciation not only nourish his soul but also counteract the effect of stress by stimulating a healthy level of testosterone.

A man in love is often consumed by thoughts of how he can make his partner happy. The challenge of the relationship creates an upsurge of positive feelings as well as higher levels of testosterone. When a man feels he can get what he wants, testosterone production increases. When he feels he cannot achieve what he wants, his stress levels become elevated, and his testosterone levels drop.

Success or the anticipation of success in a relationship fuels the rise of a man's testosterone and sustains his interest in her.

Failure or the anticipation of failure in making his partner happy creates stress for a man and lowers his testosterone. The more successful or empowered a man feels in a relationship, the more his testosterone levels will increase to healthy levels. Confidence increases testosterone, and doing things that stimulate testosterone will increase a man's confidence. It goes both ways. When a man feels successful, his energy and well-being increase because his testosterone levels are normal. When he thinks that he can't make a difference in his relationship, his energy and interest drop along with his testosterone levels. That is why being acknowledged and accepted are very important to a man's well-being.

Appreciating and accepting what he does, or forgiving him for what he neglects to do, is the most supportive way a woman can treat a man.

When a man doesn't feel successful at work, or worries about problems that he can do nothing to solve, his testosterone levels will begin to drop, and he will experience lowered spirits until his testosterone levels rise again. Depressed men have low testosterone levels.

Depressed men have low testosterone levels.

This dynamic is another reason why men will often back off from a difficult problem and forget it for a while. By engaging in another less challenging activity, he can easily rebuild his confidence and thus restore his testosterone levels. With this increased confidence, he can return to and more effectively solve the previous problem.

Shifting from one problem to an easier problem to solve can help rebuild a man's testosterone levels.

The conventional, male-dominated work environment supplies an abundance of activities, challenges, rules, and situations that can stimulate testosterone production. Testosterone-stimulating situations include:

- Goal setting
- Competition
- Problem solving
- Accountability
- Risk
- Danger
- Dominance
- Success
- Efficiency
- Urgency
- Money
- Results
- Projects
- Bottom line
- Power

If a man feels confident in his abilities, these kinds of situations will stimulate testosterone production and excite him, reducing the depleting effects of stress. These same situations can be a source of depression if he lacks confidence. Developing and sustaining confidence is one of the most important challenges in a man's life, determining the difference between success and failure, enthusiasm or depression. Ultimately on Mars, there are no failures but only quitters who lose confidence. With lowered testosterone levels, a man's confidence will weaken.

Making Testosterone at Home

In all men, testosterone levels fall during the course of the day. There is a natural cycle that peaks in the morning. During the workday, a man is depleting his testosterone. When the stress of his day is over, his body must relax to restore itself. This shift is often set off by the setting of the sun. In recovery mode, he is free from his innate drive to be responsible, so after a stressful day of work, testosterone levels have a chance to build. A man can elevate his testosterone level by taking a nap or doing simple, entertaining activities like watching TV or reading a newspaper.

When a man's workday is over, a switch turns off in his brain, and he shifts to a passive, relaxed mode.

If a man doesn't take the time to recover, the stress drives his testosterone levels down. Not only does his sex drive become low, but he becomes moody, grumpy, irritable, or passive. Women don't instinctively understand this need, because their well-being is not dependent on rebuilding testosterone levels.

Often, women think their husbands are lazy, when in fact they have a biological imperative to rest. Though women produce testosterone, the hormone has little relationship to stress on Venus. Just as testosterone stimulates stress reduction in men, the hormone oxytocin stimulates stress reduction in women.

Oxytocin, the Cuddle Hormone

Oxytocin, known as a social attachment hormone, is produced in great quantity during childbirth and lactation and during orgasm in both sexes. In women, oxytocin levels can rise during a relaxing massage and fall in response to feeling ignored or abandoned. The hormone affects social recognition and bonding as well as the formation of trust between people. Oxytocin stimulates in women maternal behavior as well as sexual arousal. It reduces blood pressure, cortisol levels, and fear. Studies have shown that animals and people with high levels of oxytocin are calmer, less anxious, and more social.

Though men and women have on average similar levels of oxytocin in their bloodstreams, women have more estrogen, which boosts the effectiveness of oxytocin. In addition, the testosterone in men counteracts the calming effects of oxytocin. The way that oxytocin interacts with estrogen and testosterone is at the root of the differences between the ways men and women respond to stress.

Researchers have discovered that oxytocin lowers stress in women, but does not have the same effect in men. Stimulating too much oxytocin in a man can actually reduce his testosterone levels. Likewise, too much testosterone in women can lower the effectiveness with which her oxytocin lowers her stress levels.

Oxytocin, the feel-good hormone from Venus,
is the love and bonding hormone.

Oxytocin creates a feeling of attachment. Levels increase when women connect with someone through friendship, sharing, caring, and nurturing and decrease when a woman misses someone or experiences a loss or breakup or feels alone, ignored, rejected, unsupported, and insignificant. A woman in love has high levels of oxytocin. She is consumed by thoughts of giving freely of herself and sharing more time with her partner.

To feel good in a relationship, a woman needs to trust that her partner cares for her as much as she cares for him. This kind of support directly affects her oxytocin levels, which in turn will lower her stress. Messages from him of caring, understanding, and respect can build trust and nourish her soul while stimulating higher levels of oxytocin.

How she interprets his behavior makes all the difference. If she interprets his behavior as caring for her, then her oxytocin levels go up, but if she interprets the same behavior as not caring, her oxytocin levels go down.

Oxytocin decreases when a woman feels alone,
ignored, unsupported, or that she does not matter.

Trust in her relationships and the anticipation of getting her needs met as she meets the needs of her partner fuel the rise of a woman's oxytocin levels. This positive anticipation is reversed when a woman expects more from a man than he can provide. Her disappointment restricts the production of oxytocin.

Trust and the anticipation of getting needs met
is a potent oxytocin producer.

Expecting too much from her partner can also prevent a woman's oxytocin levels from rising. Instead of looking to other sources of support, she expects her partner to do it all. By expecting her partner to be the main source of stimulation to produce oxytocin, she is setting her partner up to fail.

There are many ways for a woman to raise her oxytocin levels without depending on a man. Oxytocin levels rise in a woman when she is helping someone, because she cares about that person and not because she is getting paid or because it is her job. When we give primarily to get, that causes testosterone, not oxytocin, to rise. When women begin to feel they are not getting enough in their relationships, they tend to give to their partner with strings. They give, but become more concerned about what they are getting or not getting in return. This kind of result-oriented giving does not stimulate as much oxytocin, because it is tinged with negativity and anger. Unconditional giving is a powerful oxytocin producer. Oxytocin levels go up when we are caring, sharing, and befriending without expectations. Just as oxytocin production increases when we are nurturing to others, it is also stimulated when we are nurturing to ourselves.

In the past, the community of women working side by side while raising their children and caring for each other presented a wealth of activities, manners, and situations that stimulated oxytocin production.

Potent oxytocin stimulators include emphasis on:

+ Sharing
+ Communication
+ Safety
+ Cleanliness
+ Beauty
+ Trust
+ Teamwork
+ Caring
+ Shared responsibility
+ Consistency
+ Compliments
+ Affection
+ Virtue

◆ Nurturing
◆ Support
◆ Cooperation
◆ Collaboration
◆ Group efforts
◆ Routine, rhythm, and regularity

At home and in her relationships, a woman's body produces oxytocin when she feels free to nurture herself or others. When she feels rushed, overwhelmed, or pressured to do everything, her stress-reducing hormones are depleted, and her stress levels increase.

Oxytocin levels begin to rebuild when a woman feels seen, heard, and supported once again. At the end of the day, the anticipation of a simple hug, conversation, and some affection can make a big difference on Venus. When a woman thinks she can't get what she needs at home, her warm feelings dissipate, and her oxytocin levels fall.

The Most Stressful Time of a Woman's Day

Taking part in testosterone-producing activities at work can diminish a woman's oxytocin levels. When she gets home, without an abundance of oxytocin, her roles as a partner, mother, friend, and caregiver seem overwhelming. When she expects to have to do more without enough time or energy, her stress levels go up. Her experience is quite different from a man's.

When a man's day job is done, he begins to relax. If he feels pressure to do more when he returns home, his tendency to relax is thwarted. With more responsibilities and less time to recover his testosterone levels, he has less and less energy. Instead of coming home to a sanctuary of love and support, both men and women today are confronted with a new stress. Women need more of their partners' time and support, and men are running out of energy. Consequently, they both have less to give.

Women considering divorce commonly say, "I give and give, but I don't get back what I need. He just doesn't care, and I have nothing left to give."

When a woman feels that her partner doesn't care about her needs, she becomes increasingly dissatisfied and resents that she is giving more than she is getting. She may still love her partner, but she is willing to end the relationship, because she feels she has nothing left to give.

Being in his presence no longer restores her oxytocin levels after a stressful day at work. Just anticipating being ignored or rejected by him can cause her oxytocin levels to drop and her stress levels to rise. Instead of being a source of support, her partner becomes another burden for her to carry. If her partner understands her needs, it is a simple thing for him to give her a hug when they first meet after work and to spend a few minutes letting her talk about her day, both oxytocin boosters. Since she will be equally considerate of his needs, she won't be too demanding and will allow him to have the downtime he needs.

Success in the workplace is important for women, but it will never improve the quality of her relationships unless she also takes time to balance her job-related testosterone-producing activities with oxytocin-producing activities and attitudes. Achieving success in a testosterone-producing activity can lower stress in men, but not in women. It is primarily the quality of her relationships that keeps a woman's stress levels down.

Now that the hormonal differences between men and women are clear, we can begin to understand how very differently we respond to stress.

Fight or Flight

The fight-or-flight response is an automatic full-body reaction to a perceived attack or threat to our survival that prepares us to defend ourselves. The response is hardwired into our brains. When we are in danger, our brains activate the central nervous system. As described at the beginning of this chapter, adrenaline, cortisol, and other hormones are released into our bloodstreams, and our heart rate, blood pressure, and respiration are elevated. Blood is rerouted from our digestive tract and directed to our muscles and limbs to provide us with extra energy and fuel for running and fighting. Our awareness becomes more intense, our impulses faster. In this alert state, everything can be perceived as an enemy or threat to our survival. This physical response is a powerful emergency defense system in life-threatening situations.

With prolonged modern stress, toxic stress hormones flow in our bodies in response to events that do not present a real physical threat to us. We are not burning up or metabolizing the stress hormones with physical activity. We cannot flee from the threats we perceive or physically fight those we consider our adversaries. Instead, we have to stay cool when we are criticized at the office, be patient spending hours on the phone with tech support trying to fix a computer glitch so we can meet a pressing deadline, sit in traffic without succumbing to road rage. Many things that stress us every day fully activate our fight-or-flight response and can cause us to be aggressive and to overreact. This physical response can have a devastating effect on our emotional and psychological states. We feel as if we are going from emergency to emergency. The buildup of stress hormones leads to physical ailments, including headaches, irritable bowel syndrome, hypertension, chronic fatigue, depression, and allergies.

Dr. Hans H. B. Selye, the Hungarian-born pioneer of stress research who worked at McGill University in Canada, identified a three-stage response to this sort of stress on physiological, psychological, and behavioral levels. Physically, our bodies go into the alarm stage, then the resistance stage, when our bodies begin to relax, and finally the exhaustion stage. Our psychological response to stress leads to feelings of anxiety, fear, anger, tension, frustration, hopelessness, and depression. On the behavioral level, we attempt to relieve the bad feelings that stress can cause. We eat too much or too little, drink or smoke too much, take more medications, or display fight-or-flight behavior by being argumentative or withdrawn respectively.

When men experience the fight-or-flight response, vasopressin is released in their bodies and enhanced by testosterone. The combination of vasopressin and testosterone suppresses the production of oxytocin, so it is more difficult for men to calm down. As a result of the suppression of oxytocin production, men do not have the built-in tranquilizer that women have to deal with stress. In day-to-day activities, women have much higher levels of emotional reaction, but at times of great danger, when men are ready to fight, it is often women who can calm things down.

Tend and Befriend

Scientists believe that our female ancestors may have evolved their own stress response to protect themselves when pregnant, nursing, or caring for children. The tend-and-befriend response involves tending to the young and befriending others in times of stress to increase the likelihood of survival. Since a group is more likely than an individual to overcome a threat, bonding is a protective mechanism for a mother and her children. While the men were out hunting, befriending other females was necessary for women's survival, because pregnancy, nursing, and child care made women more vulnerable to outside threats.

Creating a network gave women more protection and help in raising children. Working in groups enabled them to gather food and tend to housing more effectively. In prehistoric times, males were drawn to larger groups to aid in defense and war, while females were drawn to smaller groups that provided emotional and caregiving support to other women during times of stress.

Women did not have the strength, size, or muscle mass to protect themselves as men did. The flight-or-fight response would not have promoted the survival of women and their children, because they would find it difficult to fight or flee when they were pregnant and could not protect their young if they were nursing or caring for young children.

How Stress Takes Its Toll on Women

This response to stress is still evident today in women's behavior. Rather than withdrawing or becoming belligerent, women seek social contact, especially with other women, and spend time nurturing their children to cope with stress. As you have learned, the production of oxytocin is directly linked to nurturing reactions and behaviors. Situations and circumstances in which a woman is taking care of others or connecting emotionally are the most potent oxytocin stimulators.

Generating oxytocin in the work world outside the home can be disrupted by the demands of having to make decisions and set priorities based on the bottom line instead of the needs of others, and behaving in a professional manner. These are testosterone-producing situations. Though there is nothing wrong with stimulating testosterone, it does nothing to lower a woman's stress levels.

Even the stay-at-home mom's nurturing behaviors of parenting and homemaking can become stressful if a woman feels that she is doing it alone without the community and support of other women. Some women even feel guilty or rejected by working women for choosing to stay at home rather than pursue a career. This sense of separation and abandonment only increases a woman's stress levels.

Ultimately, women become stressed out when they do not take the time to do those things that will increase their oxytocin levels. To handle stress efficiently, a woman must integrate into her day a variety of oxytocin-producing experiences. She must cultivate a mindset and a support system of work, friends, and family who can stimulate the regular production of oxytocin. Without this support, she will expect too much of her partner. This insight releases a woman from depending too much on the man in her life to raise her oxytocin levels.

An understanding of oxytocin-producing behaviors can completely change the way a man interprets a woman's behaviors. For example, when a woman complains she is not getting enough support, or feels the need to talk about the problems in her life, it does not mean she does not appreciate what her partner does. Instead, her behavior may be an indication that she is attempting to cope with stress by increasing her oxytocin levels.

Talking about problems with someone you love can elevate oxytocin levels on Venus.

Most men are not aware that talking and sharing can increase oxytocin levels to help a woman cope with stress. Without understanding this biological drive, a man mistakenly assumes that a woman is looking for a solution from him. He interrupts her to give his solutions. He does so because solving problems is one of his ways to make himself feel better when he is stressed. He thinks it will help her, too. Solving problems raises his testosterone levels but does little for her oxytocin. Once a man understands that simply listening to his partner is enough to make her feel better, his testosterone levels go up as well, because he knows that he is actually solving a problem.

Stress and Sex

There is no rest for a woman, but if her oxytocin levels are optimal, the resulting lowered stress produces an endless source of energy as well as an ability to enjoy sex. Along with good communication, sexual intimacy can be one of the most powerful ways for a woman to lower her stress levels, because oxytocin is also produced by sexual arousal and orgasm.

The problem with having sex to generate oxytocin is that most women first need oxytocin to feel sexual desire. Women who are very active sexually tend to want more sex, since sex produces a beneficial hormonal cascade. Women who have not had sex for a time often can do without it, because they become too stressed. It's the use-it-or-lose-it response.

After a stressful day, the last thing most women think about is having sex. It is often the last thing on their to-do list. There are certainly exceptions to this, but most of the time stress inhibits a woman's desire for sex.

Most women, unlike men, are not interested in sex
when they are stressed.

There are some testosterone-oriented women who want sex even when they are stressed out and their oxytocin levels are low. They are more like men, who can use sex to release their stress. When such a woman has sex, she finds some relief, but for different reasons than a man.

Sexual climax temporarily raises her oxytocin levels and lowers her testosterone levels. For a brief period, she is on vacation from her high testosterone levels. Sometimes high-testosterone women have a strong desire for sex but an inability to climax or an inability to be satisfied with one climax. Though this might sound exciting, it can be frustrating for both partners. A man wants to feel he can satisfy his partner, just as she wants to be satisfied. Oxytocin gives us the feeling of satisfaction. Too much testosterone can interfere with a woman's ability to have satisfying sex. Like eating a cookie laden with sugar, it tastes good but leaves her wanting more.

Sexual activity produces testosterone in men, but orgasm releases oxytocin. The calming effects of this hormonal cascade are why men often roll over and fall asleep afterward. After sex, a man's testosterone levels can drop for a while, which is why a man sometimes feels a need for greater distance immediately following sex.

Men and women react in opposite ways after sex on account of their hormones. While a woman's elevated oxytocin levels put her cuddle reflex in high drive, the dynamic of rising oxytocin and falling testosterone often causes a man to withdraw as his hormones return to their normal balance. Understanding and accepting that men sometimes retreat after sex, when women feel the most connected, can help avoid bad feelings.

Regular and satisfying sex is one of the great gifts of a loving relationship. To enjoy this gift for a lifetime, long after the newness wears off, men and women need to be creative in finding new ways to assist women in raising their oxytocin levels. When a woman is able to relax, she can once again enjoy her sexuality.

Hormones Make All the Difference

Giving our partners what we might want is often the opposite of what will work. Men and women have many of the same goals. We all want to be safe, happy, successful, and loved, but what we need to feel this way can be very different. It is our hormones that make all the difference.

This examination of the biological basis for the way men and women deal with stress sheds light on why Mars and Venus sometimes collide. Social conditioning, parental example, and education can have a significant effect on how men and women interact and respond to each other, but how we react to stress is hardwired in our bodies and brains.

CHAPTER FOUR

A WOMAN'S NEVER-ENDING TO-DO LIST

The more stress a woman feels, the more overwhelmed she becomes. There are too many things for her to do before she can relax. Trying to do the impossible leads her to exhaustion. Unfortunately, it doesn't stop there. The more exhausted she feels, the more urgent it becomes for her to get everything done.

In a woman's brain there will always be more to do.

Stress leads to being overwhelmed, being overwhelmed leads to exhaustion, exhaustion leads to urgency, and finally, urgency leads to more stress. In this way, a negative cycle is created. When a woman undertakes activities that create oxytocin, her stress levels drop, her sense of being overwhelmed disappears, and her energy returns. When women have plenty of energy, they take great pleasure from their responsibilities. She still has a never-ending to-do list, but it is no longer as daunting.

When women have plenty of energy, they take
great pleasure from their responsibilities.

With her stress levels lowered and her energy restored, a woman is happy and proud to do it all. My mother raised six boys and one girl. My dad traveled a lot, but somehow she did it all when he was gone, and she didn't become exhausted. She was part of another generation of women who *could* do it all. But they had a different lifestyle. They were not in the business world, making testosterone all day. Instead, they had a lifestyle and diet that sustained unending energy by producing plenty of oxytocin to lower stress levels.

The Real Reason Women Are Tired

Regardless of whether a woman has children or not, her body is designed for endurance. Recent research reveals that a woman's body has almost twice the endurance of a man's. A man has nearly 30 percent more muscle mass than a woman does, but his muscles break down much faster than a woman's—at almost twice the rate. This distinction was discovered by NASA researchers. In space, men would lose so much muscle mass that upon landing they had to leave their craft in wheelchairs. When women went up, their muscles did not break down as men's did.

A woman's body has almost twice
the endurance of a man's.

This is one of the reasons a man needs to make so much more testosterone. Besides lowering stress, testosterone rebuilds a man's muscle mass. As we have already explored, it is rest that allows his body to rebuild testosterone levels.

The more stress a man experiences during the day, the emptier his mind becomes. It is inconceivable to women that a man can quite effortlessly sit and not think about things. He just needs one focal point, and his mind goes blank. This doesn't occur for women, because their muscles don't break down like a man's and rob the brain of the amino acids required to think. The more a man feels stressed, the more he needs to recover. Positive messages from his partner lower his stress and lessen the time he requires to recover.

> It is inconceivable to women that a man can effortlessly sit and not think about things.

A woman's body is very different from a man's in other ways. Having 20 to 25 percent more body fat than a man gives her the potential for lasting energy to remain active during her waking hours. A woman's higher fat-to-muscle ratio enables her body not only to make extra hormones for childbearing but also to provide additional energy. By burning the fat stored in her extra fat cells, she can produce up to twenty times more energy than a man. This extra energy supports her brain, which never rests, churning away nonstop to create a never-ending to-do list.

> A woman has more body fat than a man, and that is what gives her lasting energy.

Women become exhausted not because their muscles are breaking down but because they are not making enough oxytocin. As their stress levels rise and their bodies produce more cortisol, their bodies are unable to burn fat for energy, but process carbohydrates and sugars. In their red-alert state, they are left with cravings for carbohydrates, caffeine, or sugar for short-term energy, which then very quickly leaves them even more exhausted. The solution for women is not taking more time to rest, but finding oxytocin-stimulating activities to lower stress levels.

Body Type and Stress

When a woman's fat-burning capacity is disrupted by stress, her body type affects how she reacts. The three basic body types include endomorph, mesomorph, and ectomorph.

▶ ENDOMORPH: If her body tends to be a round shape, she will have more energy than most women, but her body will begin to store extra fat in unwanted areas when she is stressed. An endomorph feels too many people need her, and gradually she becomes more exhausted.

▶ MESOMORPH: If she has a more muscular body, she will store some extra fat in her muscles, but she will run out of energy when stressed. Without an abundance of oxytocin her stress levels rise, and she feels there is too much to get done.

▶ ECTOMORPH: If a woman is very lean with less fat and muscle than others, without an abundance of oxytocin she will experience increased feelings of anxiety or worry. An ectomorph has too much to worry about.

Most women will experience some weight gain, a loss of energy, and an overwhelmed feeling when their bodies are not producing enough oxytocin. Body type tends to determine to what extent a woman will experience the consequences.

The real reason women are tired today is not that they have too much to do. It is that they are not producing enough oxytocin to cope with stress.

> A woman thinks her to-do list is causing her stress,
> but her low oxytocin levels are to blame.

Without this understanding, women focus on getting things done rather than generating more oxytocin to lower stress. They make the mistake of assuming that doing more will finally give them the opportunity to rest. Not only do they expect themselves to do more, but they expect their partners to do more as well.

The idea that finishing everything on her to-do list will take away her stress and distress is an illusion. Instead, it is her stress that causes her to feel overwhelmed and exhausted.

How *Not* to Deal with a Woman in Stress

Men often make the mistake of assuming that helping a woman solve her problems will make her feel better. It works for him, but does not work for her. More testosterone, which comes from solving problems, does nothing to lower a woman's stress levels. What a man can do to help is assist her in creating more oxytocin.

> More testosterone, which comes from
> solving problems, does nothing to lower
> a woman's stress levels.

Without insight into the difference between the sexes, men make things worse by trying to solve a woman's problems or shorten her to-do list. Here is a typical conversation you have probably had yourself:

"I feel so overwhelmed," she says.

"Why, what's the problem?" he asks.

"I have so much to do," she responds with tension in her voice.

"Don't worry about it." He tries to calm her down. "Just relax. Let's watch TV."

"I can't watch TV," she snaps. "I still have to make dinner, pay the bills, cancel my doctor appointment because of that last-minute meeting my boss scheduled. I want to run a load of wash, and I still haven't mailed out my thank-you notes. I can't find anything on my desk in the den—it's such a mess. And I almost forgot that I promised to write up the invitations for the school play." She sighs. "I am so behind. I have no time for TV."

"Forget dinner," he says in an attempt to help her reduce her list. "I can just pick up some burritos."

"You just don't understand," she responds. "I have too much to do."

"That's ridiculous," he says, dismissing what she is feeling. "You don't have to do anything!"

"Yes, I do," she replies, frustrated. "You just don't get it!"

Instead of helping his partner, this man's casual response and attempt to make her look at the situation from a different perspective leaves her feeling more stressed, and misunderstood as well. And he feels defeated as a result of this exchange. After a few years, he won't even bother to try to help, because it seems that nothing he does works. She will eventually stop expressing her feelings to him, because he doesn't understand what she needs to relieve her stress.

> After a few years of listening to the same things,
> a man doesn't even listen or bother to help.

Men are providers, and they are always prioritizing what they must do and how much energy they have so that first things get done first. Their single-task focus comes into play. This difference prevents men from becoming overwhelmed as women do, but it can also prevent them from being able to understand what a woman is going through.

> Prioritizing prevents men from feeling overwhelmed,
> but also limits their ability to connect.

When a woman speaks, everything a man hears is filtered to determine what actions need to be taken. He constantly prioritizes and compares what she is saying with other problems that need to be solved. In the context of problems that need to be solved first or last, he is sorting out what she says as important or unimportant. If what she is talking about is unimportant in the scheme of things that must get done, then it goes to the bottom of the list.

A woman may respond to this prioritizing by feeling that what she is saying is unimportant to him, which can get translated into feeling that she is not important to him as well. This is far from the truth, but it is how she perceives it. Certainly she would agree that in the scheme of problems that need to be solved, the problems she is talking about are not as important as the big ones. But that is not really the point on her planet. Women talk for a variety of reasons that can have nothing to do with solving a problem—they could be sharing to get close, to reconnect, to feel better, or to discover what they are feeling.

> Women talk for a variety of reasons that can
> have nothing to do with solving a problem.

She could be talking about fifteen little things that happened to her. Though she just wants to be understood, he is busy dismissing these as less important than the big problems like planning deals to increase their income and improve the quality of their life together. While he is busy doing this, the quality of their conversation diminishes. Just as she has difficulty holding his attention, he has difficulty focusing his attention.

By changing the context of the conversation away from solving her many problems to just listening, one need he can actually help her with, he is able to maintain his focus effortlessly. By giving him concrete jobs to do, a woman helps keep her partner's testosterone levels up.

Often, a woman simply needs to talk about her feelings and for her partner to listen and attempt to understand what she is going through. She does not need him to solve all her problems or to help her sort out what she does and doesn't have to do. By sharing her feelings about what she has to do, she is trying to lower her stress levels by increasing oxytocin.

If she secretly hopes that sharing her frustrations will motivate him to do more for her, she is on the wrong track. Just as men should not try to solve women's problems when they share feelings, women should not expect men to listen and then make some change to solve her problems. Women need to be clear that if they are sharing, they are not indirectly asking men to help them with their to-do list. At other times, without all the feelings, she can be much more effective in asking him for help to get something done.

How to Get Help from Mars

Given the pressures of today's world and how thinly stretched women are, men cannot ignore the new burden that women carry. Without a doubt, women need more support today. Giving the kind of support their fathers gave to their mothers is no longer an adequate contribution from men. Even so, a woman needs to remember what makes her partner feel good to get more from him.

I first experienced the importance of this simple concept one day when my wife asked me to pick up three of my shirts lying by the side of our bed and to put them in the clothes hamper. I was happy to comply.

"See how much better that looks." She smiled with pleasure. "Thanks for cleaning up the bedroom."

I felt a great sense of pride, as if I alone had cleaned up the entire bedroom.

Easy victories motivate a man to do more.

Having given me complete credit for the job had a dramatic effect. It was twenty years ago, and I still remember how I felt. The increased testosterone I experienced from being appreciated for cleaning the bedroom motivated me to continue to help out, doing more and more around the house. Her simple delight and acknowledgment reminded me of how I felt in the beginning of the relationship, when I could do no wrong and I received so much appreciation. This easy victory in making her happy boosted my testosterone, giving me more energy and drive, and motivated me to do more and feel more connected with her.

When a man can do little things and get a big response,
he gets the energy and the drive to do more.

Without knowing how testosterone levels affect a man's sense of well-being, a woman might read this example and think that men are needy little children. After all, a woman doesn't need acknowledgment for everything she does around the house. She just wants help. Without understanding our hormonal differences, she would either overlook his need to be acknowledged, or be dismissive of it.

Men can misjudge a woman's behavior in a similar way. When a man does not understand a woman's need for oxytocin to relax, he might think a woman is too demanding when she seeks to have more intimacy. Her oxytocin-oriented need for more compliments, attention, affection, and hugs could easily be overlooked or judged as too needy. By understanding the hormonal roots of our behavior, we can begin to recognize why our attempts to support our partners in the past have not worked.

Giving Less to Get More

When a woman is stressed, she often makes the mistake of giving more instead of focusing on herself to get what she needs. Just as a man needs to rest and recover after a day of action and challenge, a woman needs to balance her hectic day by taking time during her day to receive the support she needs. Giving can only stimulate optimal oxytocin levels when a woman feels she is also receiving love, support, and affection as well.

When a woman feels supported, her oxytocin levels rise. On this foundation, she can continue to give and keep her stress levels down. Though this is a perfect cycle for increasing fulfillment, it can also go the other way.

When she is not getting what she needs, her brain remembers that giving more makes her feel better. Unless she makes a deliberate effort, she will feel a compulsive urge to give more instead of allowing herself to receive.

When a woman is not getting what she needs,
she feels an urge to give more.

Unless she learns to put on the brakes, she can easily run herself into the ground. This is not true on Mars. A man loves her more when she does not feel she is making a sacrifice and when she accepts what he has to give. As she gets better at receiving the support he offers, a man feels increasingly successful.

Unless she learns to put on the brakes, she can
easily run herself into the ground.

"Giving less" is easy for a man but not so easy for a woman. To produce oxytocin, a woman needs to feel as good about receiving as she does about giving. Learning to say no to the demands of the world is just as important as being able to say yes. Since saying no to the needs of others is difficult for a woman, she can change her perspective by seeing that she is not saying no to others but yes to herself. By receiving more, she will be able to give from her heart without any resentment or feelings of self-sacrifice.

One common fear women have is that if they stop giving to take time for themselves, men will not love them. This is just not true. Men will always love a satisfied, fulfilled woman. As women realize this distinction, they can relieve themselves of the added burden of making a man happy.

When Sacrifice Is Good

All this is not to say that we should not make sacrifices for those we love. When a sacrifice is a burden, we can call that a negative sacrifice, but when a sacrifice is worthwhile, it is a positive sacrifice. A positive sacrifice is a wonderful and loving action. The word *sacrifice* is derived from the Latin root "to make sacred." By putting aside our own wishes in order to support another, we make that person more special and grow in our ability to love.

To sacrifice is to make our partner
special or sacred.

I can still remember the tremendous love I felt when I used to get up in the night to comfort my children when they were sick or crying. I had sacrificed a good night's sleep, but it didn't feel like a burden. It was a positive sacrifice. I gave up what I wanted to do for a good cause. In that process, I grew in my capacity to love my children, myself, and my life.

Adjustments and compromises are needed to make a relationship work—and men are as happy to make them as women. If we remember that men are from Mars and women are from Venus, negative sacrifices can be easily transformed into positive or worthwhile sacrifices.

If I want to drive fast, and my wife wants me to slow down, I might feel that I have to sacrifice my need for speed for her need for safety. I might even feel controlled and resist a compromise. Driving fast might lower my stress levels, but it actually raises hers. I am happy to understand what she needs so that I can make a positive sacrifice as an expression of love and consideration. I don't have to give up driving fast entirely. When I'm driving with her, I need to slow down a bit.

If I understand that my action is increasing her stress, the sacrifice becomes reasonable and worthwhile. As a result, slowing down becomes a positive sacrifice, a simple adjustment on my part because I care about her. What may have seemed like a nagging request takes on new meaning, because I understand what Bonnie needs to reduce her stress.

Understanding our different needs to cope with stress
helps to make sacrifices become worthwhile.

It is only reasonable to respect her different need if I am doing the driving, and she is sitting in the front seat. Just because her comfort zone in a car is different from mine, it doesn't mean that she doesn't trust me as a driver or that she is trying to control my behaviors. To lower her stress levels, she simply has a greater need for safety. Despite my initial grumbling response, this gesture can make me feel like a hero.

A man's desire to make a woman happy is greatly underestimated by women, because women have such different motivations. A woman's happiness and energy levels come from the oxytocin-producing acts of nurturing and being nurtured, while a man's happiness and energy levels come primarily from the testosterone-producing act of making a difference.

Whatever makes a man feel successful
will grab his attention and give him energy.

Making a Man Happy Is Easier Than You Think

There is truth behind the maxim, "A man's best friend is his dog." A dog is always happy to see him. A man may have had a frustrating day, but at least his dog has no complaints. When he arrives home, the excitement and enthusiasm of his dog's welcome lets him know, once again, that he is a hero. All a man has to see is his dog's tail wagging, and his stress levels begin to decrease.

Whenever I arrive home, my dog is overjoyed to see me and will proceed to the family room, announcing my arrival with great glee and excitement. The returning and sometimes wounded hero has arrived. This exuberant response helps to make it all worthwhile. This is the way men want to be loved. A dog's unconditional love and abundant appreciation mean a lot to a man. Understanding why a man bonds so deeply with his dog can illuminate the nature of men and their affections.

Men need love just as much as women,
they just need it in different ways.

The success of a man's actions and decisions is what increases testosterone and makes him feel good. That is why his dog's enthusiasm at his return is so pleasing to him. A dog's unquestioning loyalty and unrestrained appreciation make him feel as if he is being greeted by an entire cheering section after a major victory.

A man's sense of self-esteem
is centered around what he can do.

Acknowledgment of their actions and achievements is important to women, but this acknowledgment does not reduce their stress. Women often wonder why men make such a big deal of taking credit for things. Being appreciated for what he has achieved stimulates a man's testosterone production. Women don't readily relate to the importance of taking credit, because doing so does not lower their stress levels.

Both men and women deserve more credit
for all that they do, but this credit doesn't
lower a woman's stress levels.

This simple difference explains why men tend to avoid asking for directions in the car or put off getting medical help unless absolutely necessary. Women are much more open to asking for this kind of support. A man will ask for help, but only after he feels he has done everything he can on his own. In this case, asking for help can be testosterone-producing, because it becomes the way he solves the problem. His timing is just different from a woman's. He first wants to try to do it himself.

A man will ask for help, but only after he feels
he has done everything he can on his own.

When I ask men in my seminars if they stop to get directions, most of them raise their hands. The women in the audience often laugh in disbelief. The truth is, men ask for directions all the time. They just do it when their partners are not around. In the car, she senses that he needs help long before he does. This adds extra motivation for him to prove to her that he is not lost and that he can save the day.

Getting help is more important to women, because it is an oxytocin-producing event. Someone offering to help her can put a big smile on her face. She is getting that support she needs. On Venus, the quality of relationships counts much more than how successful you are. In hormonal terms, the oxytocin produced from doing things together with others is more important to a woman than the testosterone produced by achieving things on your own.

In our romantic relationships, a man's deepest desire is to make his partner happy. Biology predisposes men to want to make something happen and women to want to be affected. A man does not spend his life looking for someone to love him. Instead, he looks for someone he can be successful in loving.

A man looks for someone he can
be successful in loving.

In this way, men and women are a perfect fit. She is happiest when he attempts to meet her needs, and he is happiest when he is successful in meeting her needs. With this kind of support a woman is released from the burden of her never-ending to-do list. Although there will never be a time when she doesn't have more to do, his support comforts her so that she has endless energy and she doesn't feel alone.

With this kind of support, she is able to relax and enjoy the many responsibilities of her life as well as appreciate the many ways he supports her. He is happy knowing that he can contribute to her fulfillment without her having to complete her never-ending responsibilities. Understanding this distinction can make a world of difference in our relationships, reducing tension and promoting peace.

CHAPTER FIVE

THE 90/10 SOLUTION

When a woman's oxytocin levels are low, it is only natural for her to seek out the support she needs at home to relieve stress. The problem with this picture is that women expect their partners to provide that support. For thousands of years, women did not rely on men to generate most of the oxytocin support they need. They counted on the help of women in their community, while their husbands hunted or later earned a living.

Historically, men have provided only a small percent of the support that women need. The man has been a provider and protector. Though men still hold that role, it is not as significant, because women can provide for and protect themselves.

In fact, a man can fulfill only a small portion of the support women need to cope with the stresses they face today. Imagine a woman's need for oxytocin to be a well that needs to be filled; a man can only fill about 10 percent. The rest of the well is her responsibility to fill. When a woman is already almost full, a man is naturally highly motivated to bring her to the top. On the other hand, if the well is empty, and he provides his 10 percent, she is still quite empty. It feels to both that he has not made much of a difference. By taking 90 percent responsibility for their own happiness and expecting only 10 percent from men, women can set up themselves and their partners for much greater success in the relationship. Remembering this 90/10 metaphor can help you create realistic expectations for yourself and your partner.

Men can fulfill only a small portion of the
support women need for oxytocin production.

A man can stimulate the production of more oxytocin in a woman, but only when she is also taking responsibility to get what she needs in other ways. Instead of looking to a man to fulfill most of her needs, a woman must adjust her expectations. This attitude makes a huge difference in the dynamics of men and women in a relationship.

When a woman is already almost full,
a man is highly motivated to bring her to the top.

If her well is almost full, and he does his 10 percent, it makes a big difference in how she feels. When she goes from feeling good to feeling great, she gives him full credit, and he feels great as well. When doing little things for her makes a big difference, that automatically motivates a man to do more little things. This sense of success lowers his stress levels, stimulates his interest in the relationship, and produces increased energy he can put into being romantic.

When doing little things for her makes a difference,
a man does more little things.

Letting Him Top Her Off

Just as it is unrealistic to expect women to do all that their mothers did *and* hold down a job, it is just as unrealistic to expect men to compensate for the additional burdens women face and become the sole solution to the problem. Men and women can cooperate to relieve their stress, but only with realistic expectations and an appropriate sense of responsibility.

Men cannot ignore the additional responsibilities that women carry today and give only the kind of support their fathers provided their mothers, but most men do not understand what is really required. Relationship skills between men and women can help to raise oxytocin, but women also need to find ways to raise levels on their own. If she takes the time to feel good herself, a woman can then allow her partner to bring her up to feeling great. Oxytocin will increase if she adjusts her lifestyle so that she has more time to do things that she enjoys.

As discussed earlier, men are most motivated when they sense they can make a difference. Just the thought of spending time with her will give a man energy if he senses that he can bring her from feeling good to feeling great. A woman's romantic partner can only top her off when she is already close to being "full-filled." To help a man help her, a woman should do her best to get the kind of support she needs to raise her oxytocin levels. There are many ways a woman can raise her oxytocin levels without directly depending on a man. By taking responsibility for lowering her stress levels in this way, she becomes increasingly receptive to and appreciative of his attempts to fulfill her.

One Hundred Ways for a Woman to Create Oxytocin on Her Own

What follows is a random list of oxytocin-producing activities that can help a woman fill up her tank on her own. They are activities in which a woman treats herself well by doing things for herself that are rewarding, fulfilling, comforting, and involve connecting with others besides her partner. As you learned in chapter 3, oxytocin production is stimulated by tending-and-befriending behavior.

1. Get a massage.
2. Get your hair done.
3. Get a manicure and/or pedicure.
4. Plan a Venus night out with your girlfriends.
5. Talk to a friend on the phone.
6. Have a non-business-related meal with a friend.
7. Cook a meal with a friend and clean up together.
8. Meditate while walking or do deep breathing while exercising.
9. Paint a room with family or friends.
10. Listen to music.
11. Sing in the shower.
12. Take singing lessons.
13. Sing in a group.
14. Take a scented bath.
15. Light candles at dinner.
16. Shop for fun with a friend.
17. Visit a day spa or take a spa vacation with friends.
18. Give yourself a facial.
19. Work out with a personal trainer.
20. Take a yoga class.
21. Take a dancing class.

22. Walk for at least an hour.
23. Schedule a regular walk-and-talk with a friend.
24. Prepare a meal for friends with a new baby.
25. Prepare a meal for friends and family who are sick.
26. Plant roses and other fragrant flowers in the garden.
27. Buy fresh-cut flowers for your home.
28. Grow and tend a vegetable garden.
29. Go to a farmer's market.
30. Prepare a meal from your own garden or with locally grown produce.
31. Take a hike.
32. Camp out in a group.
33. Hold a baby.
34. Pet, hold, and care for a pet.
35. Take a "girlfriend getaway."
36. Ask someone to carry something.
37. Ask for help.
38. Take time to browse in a bookstore with no agenda.
39. Read a good book.
40. Collect your friends' best recipes.
41. Take a cooking class.
42. Get household help for cooking, cleaning up, shopping, and house care.
43. Hire a good handyman.
44. Plan fun family activities.
45. Make a meal a special occasion by using your best china and linens.
46. Participate in a Parent Teacher Association meeting.
47. Bake for fund-raisers.
48. Go to the theater, concerts, and dance performances.
49. Have a picnic with friends and family.
50. Plan special occasions to look forward to.

51. Join or form a new mothers' club.
52. Take care of children in some capacity.
53. Feed the hungry.
54. Read magazines about fashion and people.
55. Attend inspirational, spiritual, and religious gatherings regularly.
56. Keep updated on the lives of friends.
57. Watch your favorite TV show or DVD with a friend.
58. Listen to inspirational tapes or CDs.
59. Talk with or call a therapist or coach.
60. Study a new culture and taste its cuisine.
61. Spend time at the beach, a river, or a lake.
62. Learn to ski, play golf, or play tennis with friends.
63. Enjoy wine tasting with friends.
64. Demonstrate for a social or political cause.
65. Go to or participate in a parade.
66. Hire someone to help you remove the clutter from your house.
67. Offer to help a friend do something.
68. Take a class in nutrition, cooking, or wellness.
69. Read poetry, write poetry, and go to a poetry reading.
70. Get a bird feeder and enjoy the birds that come to feed.
71. Visit an art museum.
72. Go to a movie in the middle of the day.
73. Listen to an author speak at the local bookstore or library.
74. Keep a daily journal of your thoughts and feelings.
75. Organize a photo journal for each of your children.
76. Create an e-mail list of friends to whom you can send recent pictures.
77. Ask them to reciprocate.

78. Create an e-mail list of friends with similar political views for mutual support.
79. Take a painting or sculpture class with a friend.
80. Knit a scarf for someone you love.
81. Meet friends for an espresso or cup of tea.
82. Make a charitable donation.
83. Reorganize your closet.
84. Change your hair color.
85. Buy a new outfit.
86. Shop for sexy lingerie.
87. Share a picture album with friends.
88. Join a gym.
89. Play cards with friends.
90. Learn and practice a new diet plan or cleansing program for better health.
91. Give your old clothes to charity.
92. Send a birthday card.
93. Use household products that are good for the environment.
94. Prepare and freeze some meals for when you don't feel like cooking.
95. Take a flower-arranging class.
96. Volunteer at a local hospital or hospice.
97. Give a surprise party for a friend.
98. Give the books you have read to a hospital or the local library.
99. Babysit for a friend so that they can have some time off.
100. Take time out from your busy day to stretch.

You can undoubtedly come up with many more feel-good activities. Each of these suggestions involves sharing, caring, befriending, and nurturing. These tending-and-befriending behaviors will stimulate the production of oxytocin and the sense of well-being that follows.

For some women, reading this list is a revelation, validating and giving them permission to do more of what they would like to do. For others, it might appear to be another list of things to do. If you are stressed, you probably already feel that you can't think of doing more. Please don't ignore this list. You don't ignore your children's needs just because they can be overwhelming.

Use this list by adding just one thing to your life this week to make yourself feel good. As your oxytocin levels rise, it becomes easier and easier to add more oxytocin-producing activities to your life. Keep in mind that the reason you are overwhelmed with too much to do is that you are already doing too many testosterone-producing activities, and not enough that promote oxytocin production.

The solution is finding balance, and only you can do it. Your romantic partner can certainly help, but the first 90 percent is up to you, your friends, and your community.

If you continue your hectic life, putting out fires as they get started, your feelings of being overwhelmed will never go away, and the stress will wear you down. It is only by taking the time to learn to create more oxytocin that you reduce your stress and fully enjoy your life. If you cannot do it for yourself, do it for your partner or children. Remember, "when mom is happy, everyone is happy."

Scoring Points on Venus

Even though men cannot be fully responsible for their partners' happiness, they want to make women happy. But when women are overwhelmed, that may be difficult to do. I will give you an inside look at how women measure a Martian's contributions and efforts.

Just as men keep score in sports, women keep score in relationships. At a subconscious level, a woman is always keeping track of how much she gives in contrast to how much she receives. When he gives to her, she gives him a point, and when she gives to him, she gives herself a point.

Men do this as well, but not to the same extent, and not in the same way. Men tend to think if they do something big like make a lot of money for the family or take her on an expensive vacation, they will score a few hundred points. When he has done something big, he figures he can relax for a while. But this is not the way women keep score.

On Venus, every gift of love scores equal to every other gift of love, no matter how big or small. When he does something big, he only gets one point, but when he does a lot of little things, he gets a lot of points. When it comes to stimulating oxytocin, it is not what you do but how much you do. It is the little acts of affection, attention, and offering help that allow a man to rack up the points on Venus.

On Venus, every gift of love scores equal to every other gift of love, no matter how big or small.

A married man gets one point for going to work, one point for returning, and one point for being faithful. These are three golden points. Without these he gets no other points. These three points give him the keys to her heart, but it is doing the little things that open the door.

This is crucial for a man to understand, because men will do special things and then feel frustrated when his partner complains he is not doing enough. He may have done something great, like taking her out on a special date, which in testosterone terms scored a hundred points. To her, a successful date may have only been three or four points. Later, when she complains they haven't spent enough time together, he concludes that she is too demanding, or that there is nothing he can ever do to make her happy.

Most men overlook the little things
that can rack up big points on Venus.

On Venus, it is the thought that counts. Just offering to do something gives you a point before you even do it. Instead of just turning up the heat in my house, I will first say to my wife, "You look a little cold. Would you like me to turn up the heat?" In one stroke, I earn three points: one point for noticing her and thinking of her, one point for offering to do something without being asked, and one point for turning up the heat. By understanding how to score points on Venus, a man can easily defuse stress by making his partner happy.

If I really want to up my points, I offer to build a fire to prepare for a romantic evening. I then get more points: one extra point for going out in the cold to get the wood, one point for carrying in the wood, and one point for building the fire. Instead of building a big fire, I make it small. Every time I get up to add a log, I get a point for noticing, and then another point for adding the log.

In a similar manner, men get points for listening. Each time she covers a subject without him interrupting with a solution, he gets a point. In ten minutes of talking, he can easily get ten points. These small acts can lower her stress levels and bring her from feeling good to feeling great. At the same time, he is providing for her in a way that will make him feel as if he has accomplished something.

When a man brings his partner a dozen roses, she appreciates it, but it only scores two points: one point for him doing it without her having to ask, and another point for the roses. If he wants to score more points, rather than bring a dozen roses once every few months, he can bring one rose twelve times. This way he scores twenty-four points instead of two.

To score more points, rather than bring a dozen roses
and get two points, a man can bring one rose
twelve times and make twenty-four points.

By learning how to score points on Venus by doing the little things, men can actually do less and have a bigger impact. When she complains about how much she has to do, rather than take on her responsibilities, he can focus on doing several little things that will make a much bigger difference than the big things. He doesn't need to solve her problems; instead he just needs to focus on the little things that stimulate oxytocin.

Ways for Him to Fill Up Her Oxytocin Tank

Men get more points from giving hugs than for being a good provider. When I discovered this scoring system, I began giving my wife four hugs a day: one when I first see her in the morning, one when I say good-bye, one when I return, and one before bed. By finding her to give the hugs, I get an extra point each time for finding her. I score eight points just by giving four hugs.

By showing some interest and asking a few questions about her day, I can easily earn another ten points. Every time I ask about something with an awareness of what she was doing, I score a point. A man gets more points when his questions are specific. Rather than saying, "How was your day?" asking, "Did you get what you wanted at the marketing meeting?" shows real involvement. He will always get points for showing interest and asking about her day, but when he asks specific questions like how the appointment with the doctor went or how the pitch went at lunch, he gets more points for knowing what goes on in her life and being interested in the outcome. If he calls her during the day occasionally to ask how something went, he gets even more points.

A man gets more points when his questions
are specific as opposed to general.

As I have already mentioned, by simply listening to her talk about her never-ending to-do list without trying to solve or minimize problems, a man scores big points. Each time she talks about a new subject and he doesn't interrupt, he gets a point. The longer she talks, the more points he gets.

Taking her on a vacation is certainly worth a few points, but planning the vacation or romantic getaway in advance earns a man more points, because she has more time to prepare for it and imagine how wonderful it will be. Before they even go, every time she talks about it to a friend, she gives him a point. Every time she goes shopping to prepare for the trip, he gets a point. He can get thirty points before they leave. If they take lots of pictures, when she shares the pictures with her friends after the trip, he gets points as she remembers what happened.

Another simple way to earn points is for him to find her first when he arrives home or to stop what he is doing if she arrives later, and to greet her with a hug. He gets a point for the hug, a point for initiating the hug, and then another point for stopping what he was doing to make her a priority.

Four hugs a day is an easy way
to score lots of points with a woman.

This is the same idea behind common courtesies, like opening doors for women. It is not that women can't open doors. Of course they can. Opening the door expresses a little consideration to make her life easier. When a man walks down a street with a woman by his side away from traffic, in a sense protecting her from harm's way, he gets a point. Any time a man offers to help with a difficult, dangerous, or tedious task, he gets points. This doesn't mean a woman shouldn't do these things; it just means these are ways a man can score more points.

When a man offers to carry things, empty the trash, move things, carry the luggage, drive the car, pick up things, or fix the computer, the electricity, and the plumbing, this stimulates oxytocin production in a woman. Women tend to notice all these little things, and they certainly add up to contribute to her feeling loved and protected, which helps her cope with stress.

Whenever a man offers to help,
he gets an extra point for simply offering.

If it is his job to clean the garage, he gets a point, but when her tank is close to empty, his effort can easily go unnoticed. Offering to help with any domestic activity, particularly when it is not his "job," will produce oxytocin, and he will get points.

Demonstrating affection and giving compliments are also powerful oxytocin stimulators. When a man takes a moment to notice how beautiful his wife is and compliment her, it makes a big difference. He might think he has already done so countless times, but a woman never tires of being complimented. It all adds up.

Showing affection and giving compliments
are powerful oxytocin producers.

When a man puts a lot of effort into something, he greatly appreciates when his efforts are acknowledged. In a similar manner, women appreciate it when a man notices how she looks. She often puts a lot of energy into looking good, and it is important for him to notice and to say something. Even though he may not care about fashion, she does. If he takes time to notice how good she looks, it scores points.

When she talks, he should occasionally reach out and touch her hand. This is such a simple and natural gesture, and it is another two points. Affection means so much to women, because it is a major oxytocin producer.

One Hundred Ways a Man Can Raise a Woman's Oxytocin Levels

Men are often clueless when it comes to understanding how to meet a woman's emotional needs. Without an awareness of the importance of oxytocin-stimulating activities, he may begin to think it is impossible. With this new insight, it becomes so much easier. The little things make all the difference.

The following list of suggestions will give men some ideas of how they can promote oxytocin production in their partners. If he does one or two of these things, he'll see a change in his partner right away. Women love to be treasured. The more he does the little things, the more fun they will have as a couple. The glow will return, and he will have accomplished it.

1. Make her coffee or tea in the morning—especially on weekends.
2. Leave her a note saying you love her.
3. Give her a single long-stemmed rose.
4. Notice her new blouse.
5. Open doors for her.
6. Plan a surprise picnic.
7. Suggest going for a walk.
8. Tell her she looks as beautiful as the day you met.
9. Hug her when you get up.
10. Hug her when you leave.
11. Hug her when you return.
12. Hug her before you go to sleep.
13. Empty the dishwasher without being asked.
14. Notice and compliment her when she's been to the hairstylist.
15. Open the car door for her—at least when you are going out.
16. Get tickets to a concert or play she wants to see.
17. Take a ballroom dancing class together.
18. Go dancing with friends.
19. Encourage her to see chick flicks with friends.

20. Hire a personal trainer and work out together.
21. Build a fire on a rainy day.
22. Make a small flower garden for her.
23. Give her a windowsill herb garden.
24. Offer to help doing a tedious job in the kitchen.
25. Download or make a mix of songs she loves.
26. Have simultaneous massages.
27. Learn to give her a massage (without expectations of sex).
28. Massage her feet when she is tired.
29. Give her a gift subscription to a specialty magazine.
30. Take her to a craft show.
31. Give her a framed picture of both of you together for her desk.
32. Take new pictures of her for your desk.
33. Surprise her with baked goods or fruit salad for a weekend breakfast.
34. Pull out her dinner chair at home and in restaurants and give her the best view.
35. Give her a selection of exotic coffees and teas.
36. Take her car for a car wash or wash it yourself.
37. Wash the pots and pans after a meal and put them away.
38. Give her a gift certificate for a manicure.
39. Give her sexy lingerie.
40. Take her to a flea market.
41. Ask if she needs you to pick something up on the way home.
42. Offer to do the marketing.
43. Help put away the groceries.
44. Tell her you love her.
45. Take her out for an ice cream cone on a summer evening.

46. Give her the new novel by her favorite author.
47. Offer to fold the laundry.
48. Get a small TV or radio for the kitchen.
49. Give her a selection of aromatherapy essences for relaxation.
50. Offer to drop off or pick up the dry cleaning.
51. Take a bike ride with her.
52. Rent romantic comedies on DVD.
53. Make breakfast in bed for her with the children.
54. Set the table if she is making dinner.
55. Send her an e-mail saying you miss her.
56. Take her sailing, canoeing, or rowing.
57. Put your socks in the hamper.
58. Take her to a museum (after getting a good night's sleep).
59. Suggest taking her parents out to dinner.
60. Give her beautiful guest soaps.
61. Play tennis together.
62. Make the bed every now and then.
63. Frame a number of vacation photos or do an online album.
64. Edit a birthday video for each of your children.
65. Go fishing together.
66. Start a charm bracelet with charms for special events or travel.
67. Take her to a dog show.
68. Give her a meditation tape.
69. Ask about her day with specific references.
70. Compliment her on her wonderful taste.
71. Make a lunch date with her.
72. Replace a burned-out lightbulb without being asked.
73. Pick up around the house when guests are coming.
74. Take her apple or berry picking.

75. Have a regular date.
76. Take her for a spontaneous ride in the country.
77. Hold her hand in the movies (not the whole time).
78. Thank her for loving you.
79. Play cards with other couples.
80. Compliment her on her cooking.
81. Listen to the answering machine and write down messages.
82. Take her to a fair.
83. Toast her before dinner, no matter what you are drinking.
84. Surprise her with a long-lasting orchid plant.
85. Compliment her for handling so much so well.
86. Get an audio book for a long car trip.
87. Periodically get rid of your personal pile of stuff next to the bed.
88. Join a reading group or Internet seminar with her.
89. Offer to start a dream trip fund.
90. Give her luxurious bath oils and salts.
91. TiVo her favorite shows if she is working late.
92. Give her greeting cards or personal notes for special occasions.
93. Compliment her on the beautiful home she has created.
94. Be responsible for one dinner a week.
95. Go on a hike in a nature preserve.
96. Tell her she looks beautiful when she gets out of the shower.
97. Take her to an art gallery.
98. Give her a gift certificate for a facial.
99. Ask her for a list of handyman chores you can do for her during the month.
100. Offer to get your guests beverages when you entertain.

After reviewing this list, you will undoubtedly be able to add many more things that will work for your partner. Have fun. Remember, nothing is too small.

The Nuances of a Woman's Scoring System

At the same time a woman is keeping score for her partner, she is scoring her own behavior. Sometimes a man feels he can't make a difference, because his partner feels she has scored more points than he has. She figures, "I do more than him, so his points don't count." This generally happens when the score becomes about thirty-three to three.

As mentioned earlier, he starts out with three points for going to work, coming home, and being faithful. She gives herself the same three points and then another thirty points for doing everything on her never-ending to-do list that includes him. Every time she picks up something of his, she gives herself a point. When she makes a meal that he likes, she gives herself a point. Even when she worries about him, she gives herself a point. Women are experts at racking up the points.

By the end of the day, if she has scored thirty-three points and his score remains at the basic three, she subconsciously computes a new score. She subtracts his score from her score to get a new score. Thirty-three points minus his three points equals zero, the new score. When he walks in, he is now a zero. When a woman is in this scoring mode, I call this a resentment cold. She feels their efforts to support each other are unequal.

When a woman feels resentment, she loses
her ability to acknowledge a man's points.

If he doesn't get disheartened and keeps doing the little things, the score evens and she feels more supported. It is as though her mind is keeping track. When the score is close to even, she feels wonderful again.

Then there is resentment flu, a much more acute situation. This occurs when the score is uneven, but her well is close to empty. In this state, nothing that he does makes a difference. Before his points can be counted, she needs to take some time to fill up her oxytocin well.

When a woman is severely stressed,
nothing a man does will make a difference.

When suffering from resentment flu, she will start taking away his points when he makes a mistake or doesn't meet her expectations. When a woman's well is close to full, it is easy for her to give a man points for the many ways he contributes to her life. He may only be sitting on the couch watching the news, but she is aware of the comfort she gets by his being there. Instead of taking away points when he makes mistakes, she gives him points for trying. She appreciated everything he did in the beginning, and it can be that way again.

When a woman's well is nearly full
she will give a man points just for trying.

This shift can only take place if she is also doing more to support herself and not expecting her partner to be her primary source of fulfillment. A man's oxytocin points can only make a difference when she is taking time to fill her tank independently of her partner.

A man can only provide 10 percent
of a woman's fulfillment. The rest is up to her.

Another gender difference in scoring points is that a man feels great when he is winning. If he is scoring more points, he is happy to sit back and relax for a while. When a woman has more points, she feels as if she is losing. For her to win, she needs to feel she is receiving as much as she is giving.

The Importance of Talking

During my thirty years as a counselor, I have seen that if a woman is encouraged to talk about all the things on her to-do list and her feelings about her day are listened to, the burden of her to-do list is gone by the end of the session. Her stress is more about how she is feeling than all the things on her to-do list.

Just by talking about all the things she has to do, she begins to release the inner compulsion that commands her to do more and not take time for herself. You learned in chapter 2 that women have more verbal centers in their brains than men. During the work day, if her words are used for solving problems rather than sharing, then she will not get the oxytocin she needs to cope with stress. Women's brains are wired to be more verbal, and tending and befriending is how women relax. By talking without solving any problems, a profound change occurs in just a few minutes.

Talking without solving any problems
can create a profound change.

She feels happier and more at ease as her oxytocin levels rise, yet none of her problems have been solved or checked off the list.

Men Are Just Desserts

Taking time to talk with her partner in a non-goal-oriented manner can help a lot to reduce stress for a woman, but it is still not enough. We must remember that in past generations, many hours of a woman's day were filled with group activities that naturally produced oxytocin. To a great extent, her own life was the main meal of her fulfillment, and her partner's romantic feelings were an occasional but very special dessert. Even when a woman worked outside the home, it was generally in a cooperative community of women doing jobs that were nurturing like teaching, child care, and nursing. Today, most women face the problems and challenges of their work day without the nurturing benefits of an oxytocin-producing job or environment. Using the 90/10 principle and taking more responsibility for her happiness will not only free a woman from resenting her partner, but help him to help her. In this way, both men and women win!

CHAPTER SIX

MR. FIX-IT AND THE HOME IMPROVEMENT COMMITTEE

Men's need for space to be alone, and women's need for more time to be together, are rooted in our biological makeup. In my previous books, I labeled a man's need to be alone after returning from work "cave time." A man needs his cave time to replenish his testosterone levels, which are low at the end of the day. Just as women need more time to talk, share, and cooperate with a man, a man needs more time to recover from his stresses by having plenty of space to do things on his own, or at least to be in control of what he does.

When a woman complains about a man's cave time or his need for space, she doesn't recognize that his retreat is an important testosterone producer. It is hard for a woman to imagine her partner's need, because a man's need to rebuild testosterone levels is so much greater than hers. As we have already discussed, men need thirty times more testosterone to cope effectively with stress. Male behavior is alien to her.

Men need thirty times more testosterone
to cope effectively with stress.

Ultimately, most women are looking to lessen stress by connecting with their partners, not pulling away. Yet women can also use alone time to take a breath and finally be free from the daily pressures of doing everything. While taking a break, she should do things to nurture herself, which will elevate her oxytocin levels and enable her to relax. But this is not always easy to do. For some women, just the thought of taking time can be overwhelming. They imagine what would happen around them if they were to stop and smell the roses.

Some women, often in testosterone-stimulating jobs like banking, investing, law, or executive positions, feel the need for cave time, just like men. They are running on testosterone during business hours and need to nurture themselves to rebuild both their testosterone and oxytocin levels. They need cave time, but unlike men, they also need time to connect.

Women in high-testosterone-producing jobs
need cave time, but they also need time to connect.

Unreleased stress not only prevents a woman from feeling positive but can also restrict her fertility, in addition to the other potential health problems discussed earlier. I have so often observed women having fertility issues because they are not effectively coping with the stress of their testosterone-fueled jobs. In the last fifteen years, fertility in women has become a major health and relationship concern.

These women often cope with the stress of work by taking alone time or in solitary exercise, like running, but do not make the transition back to nurture their female side with oxytocin-producing behaviors. Many infertile women have immediately restored their fertility simply by increasing oxytocin-stimulating behaviors, therapies, and foods. For information on how to cleanse and nourish your cells to promote the production of oxytocin, you can visit my Web site, www.marsvenuswellness.com.

Just as women recovering from stress have difficulty taking time for themselves, men under stress have difficulty being there for others.

Just as women recovering from stress have difficulty taking time for themselves, men under stress have difficulty being there for others. Women enjoy coming together in a cooperative or collaborative manner at the end of the day, but connecting does nothing for a man but drain the little energy he has left. Her desire to share and spend time together does little to lessen his stress levels, but once he has released his stress, his greatest fulfillment comes from sharing, connecting, and making a difference.

Mr. Fix-It at Work

Men are naturally motivated to communicate in ways that will lower stress in men. They have no idea that this same style of communicating may increase a woman's stress levels. To release stress, a man tends either to solve the problem or to dismiss it in some way. A woman looks for a warmer, more supportive response. He thinks he is simply expressing his opinion to be helpful, while she feels he is being either cold and heartless, or he simply doesn't understand what she is saying. Let's look at this practically.

What follows is a list of examples of how men either try to fix or to dismiss the issues a woman may be talking about:

- ◆ "Don't worry about it."
- ◆ "This is what you should do . . ."
- ◆ "Just let it go."
- ◆ "It's not that important."
- ◆ "That's not what happened."
- ◆ "That's not what he means."
- ◆ "You expect too much of him."
- ◆ "You have to accept things the way they are."
- ◆ "Don't get so upset about it."
- ◆ "Don't let them talk to you that way."
- ◆ "You don't have to do that."
- ◆ "Just do what you want to do."
- ◆ "Don't let them get to you like that."
- ◆ "It's simple, just tell him . . ."
- ◆ "All you have to do is . . ."
- ◆ "Forget it. You have done all you can."
- ◆ "It's not such a big deal."
- ◆ "Look, there is nothing more you can do about it."
- ◆ "You shouldn't feel that way."
- ◆ "You have to develop a thick skin."

On Mars, these short comments would be supportive, but on Venus they can be insulting. If she is in the problem-solving mode, any one of these remarks can be helpful, but if she is upset and looking for support, they may sound dismissive and condescending.

Simply listening and asking more questions is a better male

response. Instead of solution-oriented comments, he can simply make reassuring sounds, as the following example demonstrates:

Julie collapses on the couch next to her husband, Ted, and kicks off her shoes.

He puts down the magazine he is reading. "Hi, sweetheart." He throws an arm around her. "So how did your pitch go over?"

"Can't you tell?" She slumps against him. "I feel battered!"

"What happened?"

"Well, my boss kept interrupting with questions . . ."

"Uh-oh . . ."

"I had the answers and all that—I was overprepared."

"You are so thorough," he encourages her.

"But Simon broke the rhythm of my presentation," she goes on, "and I thought it lost impact."

"Really?" Ted asks.

"Well, I felt off track. Whenever the momentum was rolling, Simon would add something, as if we were in competition, not working together. It was so frustrating."

"I bet."

"I was going to confront him about it, but I thought I should cool down first."

"Good move."

"And he did praise me to the clients."

"What did your colleagues think?"

"Nichole came to my office after and said that she noticed it, but that Simon looked like a jerk. Bob just congratulated me on a good presentation."

"You're such a pro—and you look great, too."

Julie laughs. "Thanks, Ted. You're pretty cute yourself. . . ."

Though every cell in his body wants to offer a solution or remark emotionally, Ted is doing the right thing here. He just takes a deep breath and in some manner says, "Tell me more."

When every cell in his body wants to offer a
solution, a man must take a deep breath
and say, "Tell me more."

It is this staying power, attention, and focus on what she is saying and feeling that will decrease her stress. Acting like Mr. Fix-It by giving solutions or minimizing the problem does not help. When he understands our different reactions to stress, he can see why his many attempts to be Mr. Fix-It have failed.

Women admire a man who can stay cool and calm. Women are also pleased when men fix things. Yet when a man offers his quick fixes to her emotional accounts of the day, she interprets his efforts as a dismissal of her feelings. She needs him simply to listen and ask more questions. The more she feels heard and understood, the better she is going to feel.

Men Are Sprinters When It Comes to Domestic Chores

When Mr. Fix-It actually has to get things done around the house, it is best to let him work alone, at his own pace. As I've said before, men are better suited to do testosterone-producing jobs. Projects instead of routine jobs tend to stimulate more testosterone. When it comes to domestic duties, a man can do a project in his own time. It has a clear-cut beginning and an end. This makes it testosterone-producing, and he doesn't feel as if he is being directed or managed by his partner. Most importantly, he doesn't have to depend on her to make decisions. Being out of control in a project can drain a man's energy. He doesn't need to control her, he just needs to be in control of what he is doing. This is another way men need space, the space to do things on their own.

At times a man may enjoy oxytocin-producing cooperative and collaborative activities, but these clearly do not raise his testosterone levels. Many men tend to lose interest and energy while doing the nurturing oxytocin-producing domestic routine duties like laundry, shopping, cooking, and cleaning. When men do take on some of these oxytocin-producing nurturing activities, they will generally do it in a more testosterone-producing manner and take the lead in some way, or at least have one particular function.

When my wife and I go food shopping at the farmer's market, I have my defined job—paying each vendor, pushing the cart, and carrying the heavy bags. Likewise, when I help with the dishes, I like to plant myself in front of the sink and wash dishes while others bring plates over, put things away, and clean tabletops. When I have one clear thing to do without a lot of decisions to make that involve my partner, I am more energized. Having to ask your partner each time whether this food should be kept, and remembering where she wants things to be put away, can be a bit exhausting for a man, who thrives on doing things alone, particularly if he is already tired.

When he has one clear thing to do, without
a lot of decisions to make that involve
his partner, a man is energized.

Men generally are very happy to do all the things that are not nurturing. Basically, they are happy to fix things that break. "Fixing" is testosterone-producing, while nurturing is oxytocin-producing. Other testosterone-producing domestic activities are setting up, handling, and running the various gadgets in the house, driving on long trips as well as running specific errands, driving the kids places and picking them up, keeping the garage and yard up, emptying the trash and other dirty jobs, carrying heavy boxes, bringing in shopping bags, mowing the lawn, fixing the gutters, painting, fixing the plumbing, putting things back together after a flood or disaster, handling leaks, emergencies, and disasters, and checking outside when there is danger. It is important that women recognize that these are the kinds of things she can always ask him to do; they will make him feel more bonded to her when he succeeds in doing them, and she appreciates his help.

When a woman wants a man to share in the domestic responsibilities, it can happen, but it won't look the way a woman might do it. Women instinctively want to share the process and make decisions together, but men will have a much greater need for the space to do it their way and in their time. Women don't understand this, because they have a different sense of timing and priorities. For him, rest and relaxation are almost always more important than routine duties. The routine can be postponed until it becomes a bit of an emergency, as far as he is concerned. He responds well to fixing things or driving places because these are generally little emergencies that stimulate in his brain more energy to take action.

When a man helps out in the home, it doesn't look
the way a woman would do it.

A man will generally be happy to take on projects, handle immediate requests, and offer other specific kinds of support to make a woman happy, particularly when she has a problem or is too tired to do something. To expect him to join in and share each day in her daily routines as a helper would eventually exhaust him. In this way we are very compatible; little emergencies and challenges can give a man energy, while they drain a woman's.

When it comes to domestic work, think of
a man as a sprinter and not a long-distance runner.

A man prides himself on doing things by himself. This is often why men don't immediately ask for help. They would rather drive around for an hour than ask for directions, to prove they can solve the problem themselves. To offer unsolicited help to a man can sometimes be annoying or even insulting. Men may interpret innocent suggestions as nagging, when women are just trying to help.

The Home Improvement Committee

Women tend to think they are supporting men when they give unsolicited help, since they are pleased when others offer help. Women even expect it. Helping is a way of spending more time together, connecting, and cooperating. All of these activities lower a woman's stress levels, but not a man's. Women gladly join to help in the kitchen or at cleanup time after a meal. Doing things together is what they do.

When a woman loves a man, her desire to help extends to him. She wants to help him achieve his full potential. She can become so excited about this partnership and new opportunity that she forms a Home Improvement Committee and focuses on improving him. Just as men tend to have a Mr. Fix-It approach, women tend to have a home improvement gene.

This is not the sort of attention a man wants, but she thinks she is being loving. Her nurturing hormones are at work. Doing something on your own produces testosterone; doing things together produces oxytocin. "I did it" produces testosterone, while "We did it" produces oxytocin. Men may interpret the Home Improvement Committee as nagging, while women are just trying to help.

When the Home Improvement Committee Focuses on Him

Here are a few examples of a woman's Home Improvement Committee:

- "Are you going to wear that tie?"
- "Have you eaten today?"
- "Did you talk to our lawyer about this?"
- "Why do you need to buy a new one?"
- "When are you going to put this away?"
- "Isn't it time for you to get a haircut?"
- "You should buy new T-shirts. These have holes."
- "You should slow down, you could get a ticket."
- "When are you going to clean up this office? I don't know how you get anything done!"
- "How can you think with that music so loud?"
- "Are you going to put that away?"
- "When are you going to cut the grass?"
- "Next time we should read the reviews."
- "Did you wash your hands?"
- "You've already had one dessert."

- "You are not giving yourself enough time to rest."
- "You should plan more in advance."
- "You forgot to return the DVD. Maybe if you put it here you will remember."
- "Remember to make reservations."
- "Your closet is a mess. When are you going to clean it up?"

A better way to nurture a man is to give him lots of space to do things the way he wants to do them. Rather than look for ways to change and improve him, look for things that he does right, and appreciate him. When a woman acknowledges what a man has done, she helps to rebuild his testosterone levels. Just coming home to a woman who is grateful for his support helps a man to relax and restore his energies.

Here is an ideal scenario:

"I'm glad you made it home at a decent hour." Becky *kisses her husband as he hangs up his coat.* "You've *been working so hard."*

"Hi, sweetie, I'm bushed."

"Tuesdays are always tough. Why don't you relax, and I'll warm up the homemade soup you picked up for us when you came home late last night. I'll make a salad, too."

"Sounds great. I just want to check the scores on ESPN."

"Take your time. Just let me know when you're ready to eat. I'll keep the soup on simmer and the salad in the fridge."

"Okay." Ted loosens his tie.

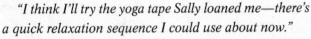

"I think I'll try the yoga tape Sally loaned me—there's a quick relaxation sequence I could use about now."

"Glad to see you taking some time for yourself. You're the best."

In this scenario, Becky allows Ted to go into his cave, shows appreciation for the big and little things he does, and manages to squeeze in some oxytocin-building activity for herself.

Men and Shopping

A man's need for space and a woman's need for time show up very clearly in our different approaches to shopping. Shopping, particularly for shoes and all other accessories, often lowers a woman's stress levels. Look in a woman's closet, and you will find rows of shoes in a variety of colors for every season, mood, or outfit. His colors for this season and every season are black and shades of brown.

Watch a man in a mall, shopping with his wife. He is dragging along, hoping the event will finally be over, looking for a bench while his partner is happily strolling, smiling, looking from left to right, taking in everything, exploring all the new fashions and discovering what is new that might decorate her house or support her children, a family member, or a friend. All these activities stimulate the production of oxytocin. Though this lowers her stress levels, it does nothing for him. Unless he comes across a Starbucks or a Victoria's Secret soon, he may die on the spot.

Men shopping with their partners may feel exhausted as if they are wandering in the desert.

Men do shop on their own, and enjoy it. Men can obsess about cars, electronics, and gadgets. The difference is that men shop in ways that stimulate testosterone. A man needs to have a clear destination or goal. Knowing where he is going and the desired outcome is very important to him. He wants to get in and out as quickly as possible. He is a man on a mission.

Sometimes men cope with stress by going out and spending money. Doing so increases testosterone because the ability to spend money is often a sign of competence and power. A woman benefits in a different way. She can use shopping to cope with stress, because it can be a nurturing activity. As long as she has time to shop, nurturing herself can be just as oxytocin-producing as nurturing others. By taking the time to shop, she can gradually get out of the mode of thinking about others and begin to think about her own wishes and needs.

Women are by far the biggest consumers, responsible for more than 70 percent of all purchases. They like to save money, but they also like to spend it. Some women become offended when I mention the importance of shopping as a stress reliever. Even for these women, shopping can be a great oxytocin therapy. For shopping to be a stress-reducing activity, they need to make time for it and go with a more experienced friend who completely enjoys it.

Since women are designed for nurturing, they can have trouble considering their own needs. The visual stimulation of so many things to buy gradually increases her desire for more, and that can then help her to feel her own needs as a priority again.

For shopping to be a stress-reducing activity, a woman needs to make time for it and go with a more experienced friend who completely enjoys it.

Not finding what she is looking for does not produce stress for a woman, because she now has reason to go shopping again. When a man shops, he is on a hunt. He wants to get in and then out. When a woman shops, it is as much hit as it is miss. She is simply gathering what is available. She can always return later to buy something on sale or when it is in season. Even our shopping habits reflect our prehistoric roles as hunter-gatherers.

The more we understand our differences, the easier it is for men and women to get along and reduce the friction between us. Instead of expecting our partners to think the way we do, we are able to consider what is best for them. This is a never-ending process.

Many people ask me if I understand women completely, and I have to be honest and say that it is an ongoing discovery process. No one gets it right every time. When we try to give our partners the respect they deserve, our lives are suffused with a feeling of purpose and meaning. Ultimately no sacrifice is too great if it feels right in our hearts.

CHAPTER SEVEN

THE ANATOMY OF A FIGHT

The number-one reason couples fight is that they are dealing with too much stress. When our bodies and minds are under stress, we become more volatile. It does not take much to set us off. Tempers flare, and we go on the attack in fight-or-flight mode with adrenaline and cortisol released in our bodies. Without an understanding of our different stress reactions, Mars and Venus are on a collision course.

Our differences in handling stress contribute to and intensify the situation. When a heated argument is brewing, women tend to explain their thoughts, feelings, and reactions with a wide range of emotional tones. Men rush to resolve the problem, expressing their solutions in a flat, detached manner. Women are hardwired to ask questions and talk, while men are designed to take action. She can easily sound overemotional, unreasonable, and demanding to him, while he can sound arrogant, righteous, and uncaring to her.

Women are hardwired to ask questions
and talk, while men are designed to act.

These natural reactions work with members of our own sex, but can provoke the opposite sex when we disagree. Rather than being kind and caring with each other, we often release our frustrations about other things by finding fault and being impatient, grumpy, or intolerant. In this chapter, we will explore the reasons behind why we fight and the dynamics of how an argument escalates into a full-blown battle.

What We Fight About

Couples commonly disagree, argue, or fight about money, scheduling, domestic responsibilities, parenting, and sex. In each case, after a few minutes of arguing, we actually fight about the way we are fighting. This shift is where the trouble lies. Instead of staying on track, focusing on a single topic of dispute, we make our partner the problem that needs to be solved. We move away from the issue and resist our partners because of the way they are communicating about the subject of the disagreement.

Staying on topic is one of the most important ways
to prevent fights as well as resolve conflict.

When we fight, we lose sight of the problem at hand. Men and women do this in different ways. A man tends to make a woman's emotional reaction to the problem the problem. A woman makes her partner's reaction to her feelings the problem. Under stress, a woman's emotions are closer to the surface. A disagreement can evoke a strong emotional response. Her partner thinks she is overreacting and getting entirely too upset. His reaction only serves to intensify her anger. In a flash, they are off topic and soaring toward a fight.

From a distance, the dynamic is obvious, but when we are involved, we don't even realize what has happened. If you are not aware of this dynamic, breaking the pattern is like trying to get out of quicksand. The more you struggle, the worse it gets, as the following example demonstrates.

Alexis and Richard are reading the paper over breakfast on a Saturday morning. Alexis is planning to go into the office to catch up when they have finished.

"Look at this new hybrid car design," Richard says, holding up the paper for her to see.

"Are you thinking of buying a new car?" she asks, with a touch of anxiety that Richard notices.

"Maybe," he answers. "This one is really a good deal."

She looks at him blankly for a moment, then challenges him in the nicest of tones, "What's wrong with your car?"

"I'm ready for something new." He takes a bite of croissant.

"I don't feel good about this." She shakes her head and grimaces. "We haven't put any money away this year."

"Don't worry about it."

"What do you mean, don't worry about it?" Alexis is annoyed and makes an emotional leap that insults Richard. "Somebody has to think about our retirement."

At this point, they have shifted gears. He has made the Martian comment, "Don't worry about it," and she is upset with him. She feels dismissed, as if what she has to say doesn't matter. Her emotional comment implies that he is not concerned about their retirement and not providing for them. Now they are ready for a fight.

> *"I work hard," Richard says, becoming assertive, "and I deserve a new car."*
>
> *"But we also need to think of putting money away." She is ready to go on the attack, shifting the problem to him. "I can't believe you are so stubborn."*
>
> *"I am not stubborn," he responds, as they do on Mars. "You are just making a big deal out of nothing."*
>
> *"I am not. All you think about is yourself." Alexis has become even more critical.*

This fight is only going to escalate. The longer they speak, the longer it will take them to make up. This can all be avoided by learning a few techniques for better communication. Men need to avoid making comments that correct a woman's feelings, and women need to avoid making disapproving comments about a man's thoughts and actions.

Men need to avoid correcting a woman's feelings, and women need to avoid making disapproving comments about a man's thoughts and actions.

Why Arguments Escalate

Arguments commonly escalate when a man unintentionally invalidates a woman's feelings, and she then responds to him in a disapproving way. When he doesn't take time to validate her feelings, she assumes he doesn't care. As she goes on the offensive, not trusting him, he becomes more defensive. Instead of coming together, they move farther apart. This dynamic is only intensified when we are tired and wound up. Stress predisposes us to be hypersensitive and defensive.

Our tone has even greater weight than the words we use. When a man argues, he focuses more on being right and offering solutions, and his tone might sound distant, as if he doesn't care. Most of the time he does care about his partner's wishes and needs, but his detached tone does not communicate that caring. When he slows down and takes more time to listen to her point of view, this conflict can be minimized.

When a woman argues, she focuses more on sharing feelings and asking questions. A woman's tone begins to sound mistrusting, unappreciative, and downright critical. Most of the time she does trust her partner's intent to help, but it doesn't sound that way to him. When she takes time to buffer her statements with appreciation for the things he says and does, this explosive chain reaction can be stopped.

During arguments, men need to ask more questions,
and women need to talk less about their feelings.

Let's look at how Alexis and Richard could have diffused their argument.

"Look at this new hybrid design," he says.
"Are you thinking of buying a new car?" She still has a cautious tone.
"Maybe. This one is a really good deal."
"What's wrong with your car?" Alexis is getting edgy.
"I'm ready for something new."

"I don't feel good about this. We haven't put any money away this year."

"I hear you." Richard acknowledges her concern. *"We could sit down and do the numbers. We'd get a good trade-in price for my car now. And the hybrid would save us a lot on gas."*

"Good points. We'll have to take a look at the cost," she concedes. *"I hope we can afford it and still save some money."*

"Absolutely, what you are saying makes sense," he agrees. *"But I work hard, and I would love to get a new car."*

"I appreciate how hard you've been working. You deserve it." She really does want him to be happy. *"Why don't you rough out some numbers if you have time today, and then show them to me?"*

Their argument is deflected here because Richard respects what Alexis is saying and takes her concerns into account. She is able to appreciate all his hard work, and her giving nature resurfaces.

Though men should refrain from telling women how they should feel, women must not escalate an argument by talking a lot about their feelings. Doing so will result in her feeling invalidated. Instead of talking about how she feels, she should stick to talking about the problem.

This advice differs from what people are generally taught. In therapy, women are encouraged to talk about and explore their feelings, which can be very helpful in raising awareness and oxytocin levels. But exploring your feelings does not help in arguments. Relationships are not therapy. Talking about your feelings during an argument is like pouring gasoline on a fire.

> In therapy we are encouraged to share feelings,
> but in a fight it can make matters worse.

Almost all relationship experts, books, courses, and seminars encourage couples to talk about how they feel. This kind of advice is greatly misunderstood. Talking about "positive feelings" is usually productive. Talking about negative feelings can be fine when we are feeling supported, but couples rarely feel trusted, appreciated, cared for, and understood at times of conflict. One of the major causes of fighting is talking about our negative feelings.

> Arguments escalate into fights
> when we begin sharing feelings.

The conflict moves very quickly from problem solving to counter-attacking. When we start pointing to each other as the problem, we cannot join forces to address the original issue. At these sensitive times, a woman needs clear messages that he cares about her point of view, and a man needs to know that she is open to receiving his support. In chapter 8, I provide a technique for defusing an escalating argument by removing emotional content, and in chapter 9, I offer a ritual that can easily be incorporated into your life to allow a woman to talk openly and safely about her feelings outside the charged atmosphere of conflict.

We Always Need Reassurance

We often think our partners always know we care and appreciate them, but this is naive. Just as a plant needs extra water on a hot day, couples need to give each other extra reassurance and emotional support during difficult, stressful times. It is hard for a woman to remain open and receptive when she feels her partner doesn't care that much about what she has to say and she just keeps talking, because she is hardwired to do so. It is hard for a man to remain supportive and considerate when he thinks he is being viewed as the bad guy when he is just trying to solve the problem or wanting to be left alone to regroup. She wants to feel as if she matters, and he wants to feel like the good guy.

A discussion can turn into a disagreement when we try to convince our partner of our point of view. What turns such a discussion into a fight is that we lose sight of our partner's need for his or her point of view to be heard and respected.

We fight because we are too focused on proving
the merits of our point of view and overlook
our partner's needs to feel understood
and appreciated.

Testosterone-oriented men typically rush to solve the problem, and women do not feel heard. Women tend to talk more about the problem and do not directly ask for what they want or suggest a solution.

The best way to minimize fights is to take more time to communicate to our partners that we understand and in some way appreciate the merit of their point of view. A woman particularly needs to feel that he recognizes and *understands* what she is saying and its validity. Men need to feel that she recognizes and *appreciates the merit of* what he is saying.

To avoid fights, take time to communicate that
you understand your partner's perspective.

He is more concerned about being right, and she cares more about getting what she needs. It is sometimes difficult for women to assert their needs. When they do, women are sometimes not tactful or graceful. Pointing this out to her only makes things worse.

When a man is making an argument, pointing out its weaknesses only makes him more defensive. If she can take the time to recognize why what he is saying makes sense, he will be more open to compromise.

For example, she could say to him, "That makes sense to me, are you saying . . . ?" Or he could say to her, "I think I understand. Are you saying . . . ?" Taking time to reflect on what someone is saying, which is easily overlooked in arguments, is one of the best ways to make sure both people are getting what they need.

Having a disagreement in a loving relationship is not a debate in which one side is trying to be right and prove the other is wrong. An argument does not carry the judgment that one is good and the other is bad. It is not a competition in which one is trying to win and make the other lose.

Arguments can be resolved when
they are not debates, trials, or competitions.

When we have different points of view or conflicting needs, an argument begins to feel like a debate, a trial, or a competition, which is not a productive tendency. We have to stay on each other's side. The need to expend that extra effort can be difficult to remember and to execute when our stress levels are high.

Negotiation of conflict requires not only love
but flexibility as well.

When couples have different points of view, resolution is best achieved by following these three steps:

1. Take the time to communicate you understand the other point of view.
2. Gauge how important this particular battle is to you and to your partner. If the issue is not as significant to you as it is to your partner, be ready to resolve the conflict. Wisdom is yielding to your partner's needs when the issue is much more important to him and less so to you.
3. A compromise is required if you both can't get what you need.

Fourteen Common Mistakes Women Make in a Fight

Considering our own role in promoting an argument can defuse many of our negative emotions and make us much more willing to find compromise. Women can recognize how they contribute to a conflict by looking over the following list of common mistakes women make. This reflection is designed to help women recognize that they are not the only ones who are not getting what they need or deserve. The defensive reactions of men will make more sense when women recognize how they also contribute to a fight.

1. **Raising your voice and using strong emotional tones**—accusing, whining, mocking, sarcastic. Try to stay unemotional.

2. **Using rhetorical questions like, "How could you say that . . . ,"** rather than directly expressing what you do like or accept. For example, "I understand and agree that . . . , but . . ."

3. **Interpreting him by changing the subject back to your feelings:** "I feel angry that you . . ." In an argument it is always better to restate what he said: "Do you mean that . . ."

4. **Making generalized complaints rather than being specific:** "You are always watching TV," or "We never spend any time together." A woman should state her needs by saying something like, "I would love to do something special together," "Let's take a walk to town," or "Let's plan a date to go out this week."

5. **Focusing on complaints rather than asking for what she wants.** Instead, you should make a man the solution rather than the problem: "I would really like . . . ," or "Would you please . . . ," rather than "I don't like it when . . ."

6. **Expecting him to respond like a woman instead of a man:** "You are in your head," "Why can't you come from your heart?" or "Why don't you open up to me?" This type of critical remark ignores basic Mars/Venus differences. Acknowledging our differences is more productive: "I understand it is difficult for you to

talk about this . . . ," or "I know you want to solve the problem . . ."

7. **Comparing him to another or how he was in his past:** "You used to be much more affectionate," or "Nobody else I dated did that." Instead, you should appreciate what he does do: "I love it when you . . ."

8. **Starting a fight to express feelings that have been building up:** "You never help," or "You always leave your dishes in the sink." You will learn in chapter 9 how to schedule a Venus Talk when you are frustrated.

9. **Going on and on without giving your partner a chance to express his point of view.** This is obviously Venus behavior out of control.

10. **Expecting your partner to make you feel good instead of taking responsibility for feeling good on your own:** "Well, that doesn't make me feel any better." Instead, your impulse should be to help yourself: "I think I'll go run on the treadmill to relax . . ."

11. **Expressing resistance with your feelings: "I feel like you . . . ,"** or "You make me feel . . ." Respond instead by reflecting what he said: "So you are saying that . . ."

12. **Bringing up old issues to make your point:** "This is just how I felt when you . . ." Don't muddy the disagreement by using your emotional memory as a bludgeon.

13. **Being unwilling to forgive until he changes, apologizes, or suffers long enough.** Understanding your partner's needs should enable you to be generous in your love. Waiting for your partner to make a change before opening your heart makes it more

difficult for your partner to make a positive change. Opening your heart and then asking for what you want is much more effective than passively waiting for your partner to change.

14. **Making demands rather than expressing preferences.** "You have to do it this way," or "You shouldn't do it like that." Instead you could say the same thing as a preference: "I would like you to do it this way," or "This way works best for me. Would you please do it like this?"

You don't have to wait until you have a fight to reflect on this list. One way to avoid fights is to find a time when you are feeling good about yourself and then read over the list and rate yourself. Find out which common mistakes you make and imagine having a fight without making them. This kind of mental role-playing is very powerful. Musicians and athletes use mental role-playing to train their subconscious minds so that they spontaneously act and react in a particular manner.

This list helps men as well as women. Before considering the mistakes that they make when they fight, it is helpful for men to look over the list of common mistakes women make when they fight. Men are better able to take responsibility for their mistakes when they understand what goes on outside themselves. It is how their brains function.

It is equally important for women to familiarize themselves with the mistakes made on Mars during a fight. Being aware of how men fight will help a woman validate her feelings and remember that these mistakes are common on Mars. This way a woman does not have to take her partner's behavior so personally.

Men can resolve their feelings easily if they can create in their minds a clear picture of what happened that didn't work and what will work. This list of common mistakes men make while fighting will help a man reflect on what he regrets or how he could have done things differently.

Fourteen Common Mistakes Men Make in a Fight

1. **Raising your voice or becoming cold, sharp, or distant in tone.** Since men's voices are deeper than women's, your voice can seem threatening and overwhelming when you are angry. Men can care so much about being right that they don't realize their tone can sound uncaring from her point of view. A woman tends to take this uncaring tone personally, as if he doesn't care about her.

2. **Making condescending comments** like, "Don't worry about it," or "You are making a big deal out of nothing." Instead, acknowledge her feelings: "I see that you are anxious . . ."

3. **Interrupting her with arguments to invalidate her feelings or correct her observations:** "You shouldn't feel that way," or "But that is not what happened." Reflect on what she has said, instead: "I understand you think that . . ."

4. **Justifying your action by making her interpretation wrong:** "But that is not what I meant," or "You have the wrong idea." Instead rephrase your point: "Let me put it another way . . ."

5. **Criticizing or putting her down by clarifying what you are saying:** "That is not the point," or "Can't you see . . . ?" or "Isn't it obvious that . . . ?" Restating the point can help: "What I mean is . . ."

6. **Expressing frustration with the pace of the argument:** "Why do we have to go over this again and again?" or "I have already said that . . ." You could say, "I understand you need to absorb what I am saying," and then suggest taking a time-out.

7. **Offering solutions instead of asking more questions:** "You should do this . . . ," or "All you have to do is . . ." Instead ask, "What do you think we should do next?"

8. **Correcting her priorities instead of supporting her values:** "You don't need to . . . ," or "It is not important to . . ." You could say, "I see why this matters to you."

9. **Minimizing her feelings instead of saying nothing and simply listening:** "You shouldn't get so upset," or "This doesn't have to be such a big deal." You don't realize that you are actually making a big deal out of her making it a big deal. Just acknowledge her feelings: "I see how upset you are . . ."

10. **Dismissing her feelings while trying to end the conversation:** "I got it, you want . . . ," or "Okay, I got it. Can we now just forget it?" or "Can we now put it to rest?" Instead you could say, "I think I understand. What you are saying is . . . Is that correct?"

11. **Having to have the final word.** Whatever she says, you come back with something to conclude: "So once again, everything has to be the way you want it." It is much more productive to reflect what she said back to her: "I understand that you want . . ."

12. **Tit for tat.** When she complains, you come back with even more complaints about her, with an attitude that she is the one with all the complaints: "That's true,

but . . . ," or "That's nothing, remember when you . . ."
Instead validate what she has to say: "In this case, I understand why you are upset."

13. **Giving in to what she wants with an attitude that
she is being unreasonable or demanding or simply
making her the bad guy.** "All right, I will do it your
way," or "Okay, once again we will do it your way."
Having reached a solution, you should embrace it: "I
agree that we should . . ."

14. **Making threats rather than expressing preferences.** "We should probably think about getting a divorce if you are going to act this way." Instead you
could express a preference: "This is really important to
me. I would like . . ."

Though these are the most common mistakes men make during
heated conversations or fights, they can also resort to the common
tactics women use. It is a man's tendency to fight fire with fire. He
figures, "If you do that to me, then I will turn it on you."

There are bumps in every relationship, especially when we are
juggling all the demands of our lives. We have so much going on
on so many fronts that it can be difficult to stay in sync with our
partners. As you have seen in this chapter, little disagreements and
disappointments can provoke a full-scale fight when we forget how
our differences are reflected in the way we behave. Stress will
make our differences more pronounced just as our tolerance for
those differences drops to zero—the scenario for a perfect storm
of a fight.

You have learned the anatomy of a fight—why we fight and
what we really fight about. Now, let's look into the techniques on
how to stop fighting and how to make up.

How Men Can Avoid Fights

One of the easiest ways for men to avoid fights is to hold back from making dismissive comments about a woman's feelings. At first this can be difficult, because men don't even realize that they are doing it; the words that offend her in most cases would not offend him. If a couple makes efforts to avoid a fight, even if they end up having one, their argument is less hurtful and they make up more easily.

FIGHTING ON MARS

WHAT HE SAYS TO MAKE MATTERS WORSE:	WHAT HE CAN SAY TO MAKE MATTERS BETTER:
"That doesn't make any sense."	"Okay, let me make sure I understand you. Are you saying you feel . . . ?"
"You are getting upset over nothing."	"I know this is upsetting. Are you saying . . . ?"
"You are blowing things out of proportion."	"Let me see if I understand this correctly. You are feeling . . ."
"But that is ridiculous."	"This can be confusing. Are you saying . . . ?"
"I didn't say that."	"So you heard me say . . . ?"
"But that is not what I meant."	"Let me make sure I understand. You heard me say . . . ?"
"It doesn't have to be this difficult."	"I think I understand. You are saying . . . you want . . ."

(Continued)

WHAT HE SAYS TO MAKE MATTERS WORSE:	WHAT HE CAN SAY TO MAKE MATTERS BETTER:
"That is not rational at all."	"Let me take a moment to understand what you want. You feel . . . and you deserve . . ."
"Why do we have to go through this?".	"I think we have been here before. Let me see if I understand correctly how you feel. You . . ."
"You don't get it."	"Let me try saying this another way. What I am saying is . . ."

Instead of making dismissive comments, a man should take more time to rephrase what his partner is saying to clarify his own understanding and to communicate effectively that he has heard her opinion. Slowing the pace can also defuse the mounting tension. His objective is not only to hold back from making dismissive comments but to communicate what he has understood. This will help dispel her tension as well as his own.

A man's job is to listen and to
communicate what he has heard.

Men get frustrated, because they think that much of the talk is a waste of time. The belief that he is not solving the problem is frustrating and stressful, which increases his impatience and annoyance. He is wired to solve problems efficiently. Now, with this new awareness of what she needs, he can talk in a manner that solves the problem and lessens her tension. When he understands her different needs, he will feel that he has accomplished something and is not wasting time. Instead of dropping, his testosterone levels go up.

Women love hearing what they have said
reflected back to them.

A woman particularly likes to hear that her partner understands her feelings, wants, wishes, and needs. This technique may seem tedious to a man, but it is appreciated by women. Each time a man uses this communication technique, she feels more understood, and he feels successful, which, of course, relieves stress by raising her oxytocin and his testosterone.

How Women Can Avoid Fights

One of the easiest ways for women to avoid fights is to talk with a girlfriend rather than her romantic partner when something is bothering her. This gives her time to sort out her feelings, release any negativity, and restore healthy oxytocin levels. At that point, she is more prepared to ask or negotiate for what she needs in a more considerate manner.

If a woman is under stress, she needs to talk and sort out her feelings before she is able to hear her partner's point of view. After talking through the situation with a friend, possibly considering different perspectives, she is then able to make fair compromises. With a greater understanding of her own needs, she can more appropriately yield to his needs. Under stress, women tend to take an all-or-nothing approach, prone either to surrender too much or to demand too much. Once she feels heard, a woman is much more capable of finding a balanced win/win solution to a potential conflict.

Women can escalate a fight by asking too
many questions, or by talking too much
about how they feel.

Her questions tend to imply an inadequacy on his part, and talking about her feelings distances them from the topic.

Rather than asking more questions, a woman must take time to repeat what she is hearing in her own words. If her understanding is incorrect or incomplete, he can then provide her with more information. A man likes to hear a woman rephrase his ideas with a slightly different twist. He is pleased that he is making sense, or that his argument is legitimate or right.

Making the effort to fight fairly may not prevent all fights, but if you keep a disagreement contained, making up is much easier as a result. The following chart explores examples of how women get off topic by talking about their feelings, or how they ask rhetorical questions that imply incompetence or inadequacy on his part. The second column lists ways for her to improve communication and to avoid a blowup.

FIGHTING ON VENUS

WHAT SHE SAYS TO MAKE MATTERS WORSE:	WHAT SHE CAN SAY TO MAKE MATTERS BETTER:
"I feel like you are not listening to me."	"Let me start over and say this differently."
"You just don't understand."	"Let me try explaining this in a different way."

WHAT SHE SAYS TO MAKE MATTERS WORSE:	WHAT SHE CAN SAY TO MAKE MATTERS BETTER:
"How could you say that?"	"So you are saying . . . What I would like is . . ."
"I don't feel like you."	"I appreciate that you . . . What I need is . . ."
"You are just in your head. How can I talk to you?"	"It makes sense to me when you say . . . What I am saying is . . ."
"I don't feel heard at all."	"Let me say this in a different way. When . . . what I need at those times is . . ."
"I don't feel safe talking with you."	"Let me take some time to think about what you have said, and then we can talk about this again."
"How could you say . . . ?"	"You are being mean. Let's talk about this later." (Then walk away.)
"Do you expect me to . . . ?" Or "Why should I . . . ?"	"Let me make sure I understand what you are saying. You need . . ."
"Why didn't you . . . ?"	"You are right, I didn't . . . I now understand that you . . ."
"You didn't say that."	"Oh, I didn't understand what you said the first time. So you are saying . . ."

To avoid fighting and to improve the situation, a woman must refrain from challenging a man with mistrusting questions and comments. Instead she should reflect back on what he said in a positive manner. Rather than accusing him of not listening when she doesn't feel heard, she should take responsibility for expressing her feelings in a manner that he can better understand.

It makes it much easier to talk without
blaming when we remember that
we speak different languages.

Since they speak a different language on Venus than on Mars, she can't blame him for not understanding. Instead with a smile she can try again to communicate her perspective in a language that he can understand. If we can just remember that we speak different languages, it makes it so much easier to talk without the blame. If we don't expect perfection, then we are not so disappointed.

Mixing Feelings with Problem Solving

Mixing feelings and problem solving doesn't work, and it usually makes problems worse. It is like mixing oil and water—they just don't combine. This is one of the major ways Mars and Venus collide.

To avoid fights, we have to respect this distinction. As soon as you notice tension rising, you have to decide if you are going to talk about feelings so you can be more comfortable, or if you are going to put your feelings on hold and focus objectively on sharing information to resolve a difference and solve a problem.

Mixing feelings and problem solving
simply doesn't work.

Taking time to talk about feelings will relieve a woman's stress, but it can elevate a man's stress levels. Focusing on solving the problem without emotional tones will relax a man, but it can frustrate a woman. With this new awareness, we can find new ways to meet each other's sometimes conflicting needs. Instead of mixing feelings and problem solving, we can create two types of conversation—one to solve the problem, the other to reduce emotional tension by listening to feelings without trying to solve the problem. You will learn how to use this Venus Talk technique in the next two chapters.

CHAPTER EIGHT

HOW TO STOP FIGHTING AND MAKE UP

Emily and Roger have been discussing where to spend the holidays, and it has rapidly escalated into an argument.

"We've spent the last three Thanksgivings with your family," Emily says with a wronged tone. "It's one of my favorite holidays. I'd like to spend it with my family."

"But we have to travel so far just for a meal," he protests. "It's a nightmare."

"It's not written in stone that we always go to your family for Thanksgiving."

"This is ridiculous. Why are you making such a big deal about this?" he asks her.

"Just once can't we change our holiday routine? Why are you being so rigid?" Emily starts to blame Roger.

"How could this be so important to you?" He is getting riled. "It's just a turkey, and my mom's a better cook."

"How could you possibly say that? I can't believe you." Emily is hurt, and emotions are getting high.

"It's chaos with your family."

"At least my parents support both of us."

"What's that supposed to mean?"

"Don't get me started . . ."

"You know, I think we need to stop this conversation now. I'm going to read a book." Roger leaves the room.

Holidays and family can always stir up emotions—it's no wonder this argument has heated up so quickly. Emily is admittedly emotional about the holiday, and Roger is uncooperative and dismissive. When criticized, he goes on the attack and hurts Emily even more. Her response is so provocative that Roger wisely puts a stop to the fight.

Taking Time Out to Avoid Fights

Talking can sometimes be the answer, but sometimes not talking is more effective. When tension arises between men and women, one of the most important skills is to take time out.

When a fight starts, men should usually take the initiative to walk away, as Roger did. His hormones are already designed for flight or fight. Under stress, a woman is designed to talk more. When tension begins to build and voices are raised, the best choice is to postpone having the conversation until both people have a chance to calm down and feel good again.

During a time-out, he should do something he loves, and she should talk with someone other than her partner. This is very important. Sometimes when men walk away, women will follow and continue to ask questions. This only makes matters worse. A man should not under any circumstances answer these questions. He should simply walk away. If he needs to say something, he should only repeat what he said to initiate the time-out.

During a time-out, a woman should find
someone other than her partner to talk with.

To begin a time-out, all a man or woman has to do is say one polite, noninflammatory sentence, stop talking, and walk away. Get out of the same room. The tension will automatically begin to subside.

The following chart contains some dos and don'ts for calling a time-out.

HOW TO DECLARE A TIME-OUT

WHAT NOT TO SAY:	WHAT TO SAY:
"You are being irrational. I can't talk with you."	"You have a right to be upset. Let me think about what you have said, and then let's talk more about this."
"This is a complete waste of my time. I can't talk with you."	"What you say is important to me. I need some time to think about this, and then we can talk."
"I can't take this anymore. You are so stubborn."	"I want to talk about this, and I need more time to think about it. Let's talk more about this later."
"You don't hear a word I say. Nobody can talk with you."	"You are right. Let me think about this, and then let's talk more about this."

(Continued)

WHAT NOT TO SAY:	WHAT TO SAY:
"I am out of here. I will not take this kind of abuse."	"I can appreciate what you are saying. I need some time to think about my response. Let's talk more about this later."
"I feel so hurt that you would say that. I can't believe this. I have nothing more to say to you."	"You are being mean. I need some time to think about this, and then we can talk."

Once you have called a time-out, if your partner follows and continues to ask questions as you leave the room, you should be strong and only repeat, "I need some time to think about this, and then we can talk."

Most women don't recognize the importance of taking a time-out, but greatly appreciate it after a few times. Since she is not from Mars, how can she know when her feelings are pushing him over the edge, enraging him and making him aggressive? But ultimately, it is not her responsibility to protect him. He needs to protect her and their relationship. By taking a time-out, he is protecting her from the warrior within whose only alternative to flight is to fight.

A man's hormones
are designed for flight or fight.

A woman should recognize that she can't say whatever she wants regardless of his sensitivities, but she should not feel as if she has to walk on eggshells around him. In the name of honesty, both men and women are too quick to give up the virtues of patience, flexibility, and the consideration of another's feelings and sensitivities.

Many women have no idea of what sets men off. If he doesn't take responsibility to let her know he is reaching the combustion point by taking a time-out, she becomes accustomed to his angry response and can be afraid to bring up her needs and wishes. A man is actually making it safe for her to talk by taking a time-out when he has heard too much or they are heading down the wrong road.

A man is actually making it safe for her to talk
by taking a time-out when he has heard too much.

When a Woman Takes a Time-Out

It is harder for most women to take a time out, because their nature is to talk under stress. Talking almost always works on Venus, but not on Mars. On Venus, it is even against the law to walk away in the middle of a conversation. Without a common understanding and acceptance of taking time-outs, a woman can become offended and even more upset when a man takes a time-out.

A woman does not recognize the importance of taking a time-out, because her hormones under stress are so different. For her, talking about something and being heard, making a connection, will stimulate oxytocin and lower her stress levels. Her natural tendency is to talk more at these times. What she does not grasp is that talking can sometimes intensify her partner's frustration and anger. If he feels she is making him out to be in the wrong or trying to control him, he can get angrier and more upset.

Talking more can be like pouring gas
on the fire of a man's frustration and rage.

When a woman takes a time-out, she needs to think things through by talking with a friend, a therapist, a relationship coach, or a support group of other women, or to write her feelings in a journal, or to pray. In these ways, she can gradually explore her emotions, sorting out her thoughts to identify her needs and positive feelings. With more positive feelings and a clear awareness of what she needs, she is better equipped to communicate her perspective and hear what he has to say. A couple should wait at least twelve hours before discussing the issue again.

Taking a time-out helps a woman sort out her thoughts
to identify her needs and positive feelings.

A woman should also take time to remember that men are from Mars, and that she may be misinterpreting his actions or words. During this time, she can reflect on ways she can view or talk about the situation or conflict in a more positive manner. Sometimes remembering the good things he does can soften her feelings. It can be helpful to present her point of view to herself or a friend in a more positive manner that doesn't reject him but acknowledges the support he does provide.

Men are from Mars, so she could
easily be misinterpreting his actions.

In most cases, a woman should not talk with a family member during a time-out. Talking with family members can come back to haunt you. They hold on to all the negative feelings you may temporarily have about your partner. They are not aware of all the positive feelings you have toward your partner to hold a healthy balance. Confiding in family members at your worst moments may drive a wedge between them and your partner.

What a Woman Should Consider During a Time-Out

Here is a checklist of twelve things to reflect on before reconnecting:

1. What am I blaming him for?
2. What am I angry about, sad about, or afraid of?
3. What do I expect him to say, do, or feel?
4. Are my expectations reasonable?
5. What do I really need?
6. What does he really need?
7. How is he misinterpreting me?
8. How could I be misinterpreting him?
9. What do I regret?
10. What do I trust, accept, or appreciate about him?
11. What do I forgive him for?
12. What would I like him to say or do?

When a Man Takes a Time-Out

When a man takes a time-out, he should first do what he needs to feel better and then reflect on a better way to communicate with his partner. For him, this is a different process. He needs to do some testosterone-producing activity that he enjoys, like playing solitaire online, watching a game, or reading the newspaper. After he feels better, he can reflect on what they were talking about, so that he can clearly express his thoughts and desires after hearing what she has to say.

It is helpful for men to remember the exact words that were said and then to reflect on what was not said that should have been said. He should take a critical look first at what she did wrong and then at what he did wrong. This kind of thinking puts him in the problem-solving mode, which will always make a man feel better and make him a better communicator.

He can consider what she needed and how she could have said it in a way that would make him feel more appreciated. Doing this helps him to understand that it is not always an easy task to say things in ways that don't bother him. He can think about how he probably made the conversation worse by trying to fix her or solve the problem before taking the time to hear her. This process tends to soften his heart and to take away his defensiveness.

A man's defensiveness softens as he considers how
he could be approached in a different manner.

What a Man Should Consider
During a Time-Out

Here is a checklist of twelve things for a man to reflect on before reconnecting:

1. What did she say that was annoying?
2. What did she not say that she should have said?
3. What was she trying to say?

4. How could she have said it differently?
5. What did she need?
6. What do I need?
7. How is she misinterpreting me?
8. How could I be misinterpreting her?
9. What is the best possible outcome for each of us?
10. What do I regret, or how should I have done it differently?
11. What do I forgive her for?
12. What would I like her to say or do?

Men can quickly resolve their feelings if they can create a clear picture in their minds of what happened that didn't work, and what will work.

There are millions of factors in our lives that affect our mood and temperament. When your partner is upset or defensive, it doesn't matter how reasonable or legitimate your perspective is. Nothing you say or do will help. You must accept that for a period of time neither of you can hear, understand, or appreciate the other's point of view. At these times there is nothing you can do but retreat and try again later, but not before a twelve-hour break.

A common saying on Mars:
When a tornado comes, find a ditch and lie low.

Don't ever expect your partner to hear your point of view in a positive manner if you are pushing it on her. If you cannot hear her point of view, don't expect her to be able to hear your point of view. As your resistance increases, so does your partner's. In this way, resistance is guaranteed to intensify.

When you resist your partner,
his or her resistance to you will increase.

Another Mars/Venus ground rule to avoid fights is that he needs to hear her thoughts, feelings, and needs before she needs to hear what he has to say. Men have a greater ability to listen as long as they recognize that they are solving the problem by listening and not arguing.

As you now know, men need to fix things, and women need to talk. Once she has talked, his job to fix things is to communicate to her satisfaction that he has heard her point of view. If a man recognizes how important his listening is to his partner's well-being, he will be willing to do it. When her oxytocin levels rise and stress stops paralyzing her, she becomes capable of hearing what he has to say. When both feel heard, they become flexible enough to make a compromise if that is what is needed.

The Rules of Fight Avoidance

The Mars/Venus technique for avoiding a heated and painful fight is straightforward: the man initiates the time-out, and the woman approaches him later to schedule a time to talk. In this case, he protects them from hurting each other by insisting on a time-out, and she helps bring them back together with conversation.

He calls for a retreat to regroup, and later
she approaches him with a white flag to talk.

When a man stops a heated argument, he could say, "Let's first just talk about how you feel, and then we can focus on problem solving later." When they talk, he should only respond by making brief supportive comments like, "Tell me more." When she is done, he could say, "Let me think about this, and then we can talk later about what to do."

Either can start a time-out or later set a time to talk, but this suggested order is most aligned with our hormonal differences and will help reduce the stress of the situation.

Restoring Harmony

Now that you have learned how to stop a fight, let's consider how to resolve the conflicts that can lead to resentment and estrangement if they are left to fester. If a woman holds on to her bad feelings after a disagreement, her oxytocin levels will plummet, and that will trigger a downward spiral in her interactions with her partner.

When we fight, there are two ways to restore harmony: Venus Talks and Mars Meetings. A Venus Talk gives a woman the opportunity to discuss her feelings without any attempt to solve the problem. A Venus Talk allows a woman to explore her feelings and why she is upset. A Mars Meeting is strictly for problem solving.

Scheduling a Mars Meeting

After at least twelve hours have passed since the fight, a couple can talk about the issue without including any discussion of feelings. A Mars Meeting can happen without a Venus Talk, depending on whether or not a woman needs to talk about her emotions. In some situations, a break during which the couple reflects separately on what happened is enough. They are ready to go directly to a resolution of the conflict in a Mars Meeting. During this time, they try to remain as objective and solution-oriented as possible. The fewer words, the better.

Venus Talks Part I

When a woman needs to talk about the feelings an argument calls up, the Mars Meeting should be delayed. Instead, she could initiate a Venus Talk. She could say, "I need some time to talk about my feelings. We don't need to fix or solve anything at this time. You don't have to say anything. You don't have to change in any way. All you have to do is listen. You don't even have to feel bad."

Then all he is expected to do is say, "Tell me more."

By not problem solving at a Venus Meeting, she gets a chance to feel heard, and he can reflect on the things that he has heard. When she is done, she should say something like, "Thanks for listening. It really helps. I feel much better."

These simple words can make a world of difference. When a man has a very clear and workable job description, he can and will listen. When she is done, it is always good for her to walk away. Basically, he feels he has supported her by listening. If she then insists on his talking, it is as if he is being punished for doing a good deed.

As you will learn in the next chapter, Venus Talks have another function. Scheduled Venus Talks, independent of fighting, can be a powerful strategy to help women relieve stress when they feel it mounting.

Never rush into having a Mars Meeting to resolve a fight. If a meeting is scheduled before both partners have had a chance to reflect on the fight, he runs the chance of suggesting a solution that might not take her feelings into account, which would repeat what had started the quarrel to begin with. When they take more time, he gets to consider her feelings more deeply, and she gets to feel heard.

Always wait twelve hours after calling a time-out
to schedule a Mars Meeting to resolve a fight.

While they are apart, away from the heat of battle, they have a chance to see the situation from the other's perspective. Naturally, they both become more open and flexible, and as a result their Mars Meeting will be more efficient and mutually supportive.

This is how it works:

Emily is feeling terrible that she became so emotional, but Roger had insulted her family. He was wise to walk away from the fight before they said things they would regret even more. She decides to ask for a Venus Talk. She does a few things around the house and then finds him in the den and says, "I'm feeling very emotional. I think a Venus Talk would really help."

They arrange to talk in an hour. In the meantime, Emily calls her friend Kim to discuss the problem. When she and Roger meet, she is calm and clear enough to say, "I know you really don't care about holidays, but they are special to me. I love Thanksgiving, because it is a simple celebration—no presents and all that."

"So you're saying that Thanksgiving isn't laden with pressure?" Roger reflects back what she is saying.

"Right, it's a more peaceful holiday really." Emily continues to explain. "I know your parents live closer and

your family is smaller, so our presence makes a difference. But I really miss celebrating Thanksgiving with my family. I don't think it's too much to ask to spend the holiday with them now and then. We see your family so often."

"I see . . ."

"And I know your mother is a gourmet cook, but I grew up with my family's traditional recipes, and they are comforting to me."

"I understand."

"Your family is so formal that I find it hard to relax. I know my family is boisterous. I find it lively and fun. It hurts me that you find it chaotic."

"Tell me more."

"I think my family has embraced and accepted you in a way your family will never do for me. I know I'm talking about different styles. Your family is much more reserved. But I always feel that they are being polite to me. I feel like an outsider."

"Go on."

"I guess I just miss my family. We haven't seen them since June, and I'd rather not wait until Christmas."

"Okay, we'll figure it out later."

"Thanks for listening to me, Roger. Just talking has made me feel better."

Roger has time to consider what Emily has said. The Mars Meeting, scheduled for the next day, goes like this:

"I understand that you are feeling anxious about Thanksgiving this year," Roger begins. "You've made it clear to me that going to your parents is important to you."

"Yes, it is."

"Why don't we look into airfare and reservations?" Roger suggests. *"If we can book flights that are convenient and not exorbitant, I'd be willing to fly out there for Thanksgiving."*

"I'll get right on it." Emily is happy. *"Thanks for understanding."*

"I love you and want you to enjoy your favorite holiday."

"And we can have Christmas with your family for a change and have a cozy time at home." Emily goes on to apologize. *"I'm sorry for getting so crazy."*

"And you know I love your family and have a great time when we are there. I'm sorry for criticizing them in anger."

In this scenario, Emily and Roger are able to walk away from an escalating fight. Emily is able to voice her feelings, which so move Roger that accommodating her wishes is no problem at all. Where they celebrate the holiday means much more to her than it does to him.

Resisting the Need to Tell All

We are naive to believe that we have to share everything with our partners if we are to be close and intimate. In a romantic relationship, intimacy contributes to the excitement and sense of fulfillment, but we don't have to say everything we think or feel at once; we can pick and choose what parts we share. It is always a mistake to look to our romantic partner to meet our every need.

There are plenty of people in our lives to share the different parts of who we are. To be connected, we don't have to share every feeling or idea that we have. In a romantic relationship, it is important that we share the most loving and supportive parts of who we are.

Couples need to express themselves,
but they don't have to say everything
they think and feel.

This is one of the common failures in marriage. After years of just saying and doing whatever we feel, couples treat each other with less affection, kindness, and consideration than a complete stranger or guest. We get too comfortable with each other and stop trying to make a difference. It is important to remember how we treated our partners in the beginning and try to maintain that kind of support to some degree.

Many couples will treat a stranger or guest with
greater consideration than each other.

If you want to vent all your feelings or express your solutions to feel better, it is best to write them down in a journal or talk with a good friend, a support group, a relationship coach, or a therapist. It is easy to hear negativity when it is not about you. Your friends can listen to you vent, because your feelings and thoughts are not about them. When you have released negativity, it is much easier to share your positive feelings as well as your wishes and needs. When it comes to avoiding battles in your relationship, knowing when to hold your tongue is even more powerful than saying the right things.

Knowing when to hold your tongue
is more powerful than saying the right things.

Warning: Dysfunctional Behaviors Are Not Gender Differences

Not all differences are gender-specific. Some people get a rush or feeling of power when others are afraid of them. This is not a basic gender difference, but a sign of insecurity from unresolved past issues, learned behaviors from our parents, or immaturity. When men or women are insecure, they have an equal tendency to use strong emotional outbursts or the silent treatment as a way to threaten, shame, or punish their partners. When this is the case, they are using their reactions to control and manipulate rather than to release their stress.

Strong emotional outbursts or the silent
treatment can be misused by men and
women to threaten or punish.

This is an important distinction. A man may pull away as a legitimate way to cope with stress, or the same retreat could be to punish his partner or to teach her a lesson. A dysfunctional man could pull away because he is under stress, and when he notices how much it upsets her, he may use retreat to hurt her.

When a man pulls away to cope with his own stress, a woman may choose to punish him by pulling away when he comes back. She may develop the testosterone tendency of pulling away. Unfortunately, her spiteful behavior does not support either partner.

When a woman gets emotional as a legitimate need to cope with stress, a man may choose to punish her by becoming extremely emotional in return. This response is common when men are addicted to drugs or alcohol. They use their negative emotions as a way to intimidate others.

Men often use emotions to threaten
when they are addicted to drugs or alcohol.

Women also can misuse their emotional responses to cause distress to others. At times of insecurity, she could use her emotions as a way to teach him a lesson, to make him feel guilty, or simply to "give him a hard time." Natural and healthy tendencies can be misused to punish rather than love.

Natural and healthy tendencies
can be misused to punish rather than love.

Punishing our partners by withholding our love may work in the short term, but in the long term it creates fear and mistrust, causing ongoing tension and conflict. Unless both people feel they can get what they need in a relationship, both people will ultimately lose.

An attitude of "I win when you lose" in a relationship is an empty victory. When you love someone, you lose if that person loses. The only way to win is if you both win. The greatest pain we feel in a relationship comes when we withhold the love in our hearts. Ultimately, we want our partners to feel safe and free to be themselves in our presence.

Safety and freedom are the primary sources
of happiness and passion in our relationships.

Our ability to discuss and resolve our differences determines our success in a relationship. When differences push us farther away, our passion diminishes in time. When we can resolve our differences by means of loving support, good communication, and healthy compromise, we have a good chance of sharing a lifetime of love without having to start over to find love.

How to Make Up

After taking a reflective time-out and resolving your own feelings, you are then ready to make up. Trying to make up while you are still waiting for your partner to apologize will never work. Whenever there is an upset in your relationship, only one of you needs to apologize to make up.

There is always something you can apologize for, even if you feel that your partner is more in the wrong. Simply saying you are sorry and that you want to make up is one of the most powerful statements to make. Apologizing is certainly one of the most important skills we can learn.

Learning to say we are sorry
is one of the most important relationship skills.

If your partner apologizes to you, and you are not ready to make up, at least let him know that you appreciate the apology. At

this point, the ball is in your court. It is up to you to process your issues so that you can finally let go and make up with your partner.
It only slows down the healing process to justify staying hurt because our partner has not apologized or because he doesn't feel bad
enough.

During a time-out, it may help you to let go of wounded feelings by writing a letter to yourself, saying the words you need to
hear. Write out what you would want to hear to make you feel better. In this way, you are taking a step toward being responsible for
feeling better. Read the letter and imagine how you would feel if
your partner said or felt these things. Then write out what you
would want to say in response. By doing this, you are then free to
feel your heart open once again.

You can also give this letter to your partner and ask him to
read it to you. Let him know these words would feel really good to
you if he used them in his apology. If he can't say the exact words,
try to appreciate what he can say.

*Nancy and Jeremy are having an argument that began
when she discovered that he had forgotten to send in the
check for the car insurance, ignoring repeated reminders
addressed to him. When Nancy learns that their car
insurance has been temporarily suspended, she goes
ballistic. She accuses him of being careless, sloppy, and
irresponsible and putting everything they have worked
for in jeopardy. She asks how she can trust him after
he's let something like that happen.*

*He dismisses her reaction as excessive, saying that he
just has to call their insurance agent to reinstate the pol-
icy. Of course, she remembers everything he has forgotten for the last three years and reminds him of his*

mistakes. Their argument deteriorates into his calling her a nag.

Nancy is incensed. After thinking about what transpired, she sits on their bed with a legal pad and writes herself this letter, expressing the words she would want Jeremy to say:

Dear Nancy,

I am so sorry I let the car insurance lapse. I have had so much on my mind with the crisis at the office that I haven't been paying enough attention to you and to what's going on at home.

You do so much to run the household, and my contribution is so limited. I know I often take what you do for granted, but I wanted you to know that I couldn't do what I do without your support, foresight, and love.

Even though you work hard, you think of everything for our comfort. I don't know how you do it, but I am in awe that you make it look so easy.

I treasure the life we have made together, and I am sorry that my mindlessness put us at risk. I am sorry that I turned it around to make you look bad, when I know I had messed up. I really try to make you happy, and I get nuts when you obviously are not. Please forgive me for acting like a jerk on so many counts. I love you and want to see a big smile on your lovely face.

Love,
Jeremy

Her response to the imaginary letter:

Dear Jeremy,

Thanks for appreciating and understanding how important our life together is to me and letting me know the same is true for you. Thanks for recognizing how much I juggle to keep everything running smoothly and the support I try to give you.

Thanks for understanding that I'm stressed out and get fixated on the little things. I don't mean to nag. I'm just always racing around with so much on my mind that has to be done, and sometimes I resent your ability to zone out in front of the TV without a care in the world.

I love you and want us to deal with the demands of our lives together with more grace and harmony.

Love,
Nancy

If you can't agree on what went wrong or who is wrong, agree that what happened is not what you wanted to happen, and that you want to make up and feel connected again.

Emotional wounds are like physical wounds. We bruise, but we also heal. If we are waiting for our partners to provide us with a specific apology to help us heal, we are postponing our healing. A child needs to hear an apology, but an adult can gradually learn to let go on his own. As adults, it is important to learn how to open our hearts again without waiting for our partners to take that step.

CHAPTER NINE

TALKING ABOUT FEELINGS IN A FIGHT-FREE ZONE

For many men, the worst thing a woman can say is, "We need to talk." This should be the best thing she could say, but since we are so often not on the same page when we talk, a conversation either exhausts a man or it turns into a fight.

In the work world, feelings are always put on the back burner. It is not appropriate to talk about your feelings with a customer or client. We are there to serve by getting the job done. At home and in relationships, it is a different matter. By the time women get home, they are starved for some oxytocin-producing experiences.

Since feelings are put on a back burner at work,
women need to bring them forward at home.

When a woman doesn't get the time she needs to talk about her feelings, she is cut off from one of the most powerful ways for her to lower stress. If women are to spend their days at work or isolated in their homes, they need to balance the increased testosterone that comes with feeling so responsible with increased oxytocin.

Often, a woman's biggest complaint in her relationship with a man is that he doesn't listen. This scenario became relevant only recently, as her lifestyle now prevents her from having a community of other women with whom to share. In the past, women spent their days in the company of other women. They did not expect men to listen to the nuances of their feelings and reactions.

In the past, men have never
been required to be good listeners.

When women don't get a chance to talk throughout the day, they become stressed. When a woman returns home, she needs to share her feelings with her partner. If her need is not met, whatever else he does for her is experienced through a filter that says she is not getting enough from him.

When couples don't talk,
nothing he does is ever good enough.

As you know from previous chapters, when couples do talk, it can't be the way women share with each other, because a man is not a woman. If you follow the strategies and techniques in this chapter, talking with a man can be even more stress-reducing than sharing with another woman, particularly during a Venus Talk.

Talking about Feelings at All the Wrong Times

Women often sabotage their success in relationships by bringing up their feelings at inappropriate times. Single and married women will do the same thing. A woman will unconsciously start arguments or express complaints about something just to find a way to release her feelings. If something goes wrong, she will happily discuss it in great detail just to talk about her feelings.

> Women on a date will complain
> too much just to make conversation.

She may be distressed about her job, but when he takes her out on a date, she talks about how bad the food is or what a mistake it was to eat out. He could simply ask her to pick up something at the cleaners, and she bursts into a description of how much she has to do when a simple "I'm too busy" would suffice.

> Women can go on and on when a simple
> "no" is more than enough information.

Going on and on is her misguided attempt to stimulate oxytocin production to release stress. The time a woman chooses to express her feelings affects whether a man is capable of listening. Timing is everything in life and in communication. When a woman is stressed at home, she loses her sense of timing.

Here are a few examples of bad timing and how men may react:

WHAT SHE SAYS:	HOW HE FEELS:
If she disapproves of his parenting style, she will wait to bring it up until the children are not cooperating, not happy, or not doing well.	He feels blamed and criticized at a time when he is most vulnerable. Not only is she being unsupportive, but he feels she doesn't appreciate his efforts to be a good parent.
If she is overwhelmed, she will wait until he asks her to do something, and then she will complain in great detail that she is already doing too much.	He feels blamed, as if he is wrong for asking for help, and he feels burdened by her problems. He feels as if he has let her down in some way and that her problems are his fault.
If she is upset that he is not doing what he said, she will wait until he is happily engaged in some relaxing or entertaining activity like reading a book or watching TV.	He feels annoyed that she waits until he is taking his needed recovery time and then expects him to stop and respond to her needs. He wants to respond, but he has to rest. He feels she is making demands.
If she wants to spend more time with her partner, she will wait until he wants to spend time with a friend and then decide to talk about her feelings.	He feels manipulated by her feelings. When he wants to take care of his own needs, she becomes needy. He cares about her feelings, so to meet her needs he can't do what he wants to do.

At these times, when a woman insists on talking about her feelings, wishes, and needs, a man may assume she is trying to control him. Usually, she is just looking for ways to bring up subjects he doesn't seem interested in talking about. With regular opportunities to talk, this tendency in women disappears.

The chart above demonstrates how on Mars it may seem as if she is just waiting to reject, criticize, complain, control, or punish her partner. After a closer look, you begin to realize what is obvious to any woman living with a man. There are very few opportunities to share her feelings with her partner in the course of their busy days. When an opportunity presents itself, those feelings just come up. At these times, men have to remember that women are hard-wired differently, and that this is the way they respond to stress.

The solution to this problem, beyond simply accepting this difference, is to create times to talk. Even though he may have nothing to say, she can talk, and all he has to do is listen. If he is expected to do more, it can be excruciating to have a conversation.

Creating Time for a Woman to Talk about How She Feels

Creating times just to talk generally doesn't work, because men have little to say. When he understands he is not expected to share, a man is much more willing to talk with his partner. If it can make her happy and it doesn't require him to be someone he is not, then he is willing to do it.

If talking means she talks, and he listens to support her in feeling better, he can easily do that. If talking means she talks about her feelings and then expects him to talk about his feelings, it is another story. If she plans to talk about her feelings and also attempt to solve problems, the prospect is even more off-putting to a man.

Women want to talk about feelings and solve problems at the same time. This is how they do it with their girlfriends, and this is how they want to do it at home. Expecting her partner to talk like a girlfriend sets a woman up for disappointment, and sets him up for failure. If she wants to solve problems with him, she needs to speak his language and remove the overlay of feelings.

In the past, women rarely went to men to talk about their feelings. It is only with the advent of therapy that women have expected men to explore and validate their feelings while also solving problems. This expectation is unrealistic and can cause serious friction in relationships.

At these times, it is not only smart but also an act of loving compassion and kindness for a man to prioritize a woman's need to talk about her feelings before focusing on solving problems. By recognizing that this action will help her feel better, he is solving a potentially explosive problem and keeping his testosterone levels raised at the same time.

It is always best to focus on feelings first,
before trying to solve problems.

Without understanding this, a man's testosterone levels would drop when he passively listens to his partner's feelings or her resistance to his action plans. Just listening to her feelings seems a no-win situation. When women talk about problems, men start to become restless, irritable, and then depressed. When he responds to her with these symptoms of resistance, she feels even more stressed. To prevent this friction from escalating into a fight, men need to learn the art of listening without interrupting to solve her problems.

When women talk about problems,
men become restless, irritable, and then depressed.

This approach does not give a woman free rein to say whatever she wishes while a man is expected to listen passively. By being considerate of his needs and careful of what she says, she will not only make it possible for him to listen but will create more oxytocin for herself. When she can trust that he will hear what she has to say, her stress will be reduced.

Venus Talks, Part II

Unfortunately, despite cell phones and text messaging, the pace and demands of our lives have deprived many women of the opportunity to vent with a friend on a regular basis. Venus Talks help fill this void very efficiently. To help women cope with the stress of not being able to talk freely during the day, men can listen without any intention to fix and solve. Meanwhile, the woman talks without the intention to solve her problems, other than her basic need to bond. In this way she can share the details of her day without any specific desired outcome. When she simply shares her day, her oxytocin levels will begin to rise.

Women need help to remember
how to talk in a way that produces oxytocin.

Just as men need to learn to listen, women need to practice sharing without expecting him to change in some way. If while sharing she also wants to teach him a lesson, improve his behavior, or make him feel bad, it will backfire. She would be using her negative feelings to motivate or change his behaviors. As a result he would feel manipulated by her feelings and emotions and eventually be more resistant to listening.

Sharing without intending for him to change or do something about her problems and challenges can be difficult, because all day long she is in the testosterone mode of solving problems. Yet by doing so, she shifts back to producing big doses of oxytocin and counteracts a full day of rising testosterone.

Claire's Bad Day

Claire needs to clear her head after a day in which everything has gone wrong. She is glad it is the night of one of their regularly scheduled Venus Talks. She and Al talk after he watches the nightly news.

"Everything went wrong today," Claire begins. "You wouldn't believe it. It really threw me."

"Tell me about it," he responds.

"Well, on the way to the office, I had stopped at the post office to send that package to my niece . . ."

"Nice."

"I was about to pull into a space when a woman talking on the phone in her SUV came from the other direction and just cut me off."

"You're kidding . . ."

"No, it was as if she owned the world. So I opened my window and said to her as she was getting out, 'Excuse me, I was pulling into that space.'"

"What did she do?"

"She just ignored me."

"No!"

"Yes. She just rushed off. I was so upset I just skipped the whole thing."

"That's awful."

"People are so rude."

"Then what happened?"

"So I felt so shaken that I decided to treat myself to a cappuccino. There were long lines, but I decided to wait."

"Uh-huh."

"As I was getting into the car, I managed to spill the whole thing on my good coat and my oyster-colored slacks."

"Oh, no!"

"I managed to get the stains out in the restroom at work, but I smelled like wet wool and coffee most of the day."

"That must have made you uncomfortable."

"And Jeanine made a snide remark about it at a meeting."

"Really."

"Then I heard through the grapevine that management is thinking of reducing or even doing away with our bonus plan next year . . ."

"Humm?"

"That's what the word is. I was so counting on getting a decent bonus so we could redo our bathroom."

"Mmmm . . ."

"And then my lunch date canceled. It's the fourth time Sherry has done that to me at the last minute. I worked my schedule around fitting her in. I guess having lunch with me doesn't really mean that much to her, she had the flimsiest excuses."

"Tell me more."

"I think I'll talk to her about it, but I feel pathetic and needy. Maybe the friendship needs a time-out. I'm busy, and if she doesn't value my time . . ."

"I know what you mean."

"Anyway, I could go on, but I feel less down than when we started to talk."

"What a crummy day."

"Sometimes when a day gets to a bad start, it just goes downhill, and I'm powerless to turn it around."

"I know the feeling."

"Well, at least we can have a nice evening."

Al gets up from where he is sitting and gives her a big hug. "Yep, the day is not over yet."

"You're the best," Claire said. "Just talking to you has saved the day."

This one-sided conversation is certainly not the way women talk on Venus, but it is actually a more powerful oxytocin producer. When women talk with each other, they will naturally mix feelings with a gradual tendency to solve problems. In this kind of conversation, if they blend sharing and fixing, both oxytocin and testosterone are being produced. When a woman learns to share her feelings without looking for a solution, as in the conversation above, her oxytocin levels go even higher, because her body will not be producing testosterone that blocks the effects of the calming hormone oxytocin. This opportunity helps her release stress even more effectively, and as a result she realizes that she doesn't need help to solve her problems, or the importance of her problems melts away. When she talks, and he listens, she gets many of the benefits of therapy.

When a woman comes to me for counseling, she is not speaking to try to change her partner. He is not even there. Instead, she is coming to help herself. She may want to change her partner, she may ask for ways to change her partner, but she is actually in the pure act of sharing her feelings, because he is not present, which is why it works so well.

There are two other benefits of Venus Talks that also emerge in a therapy session. Since therapy is inherently about the client, the dynamic between the counselor and client makes the exploration of a woman's feelings more effective. Secondly, when the client begins to try to solve the problem, a skillful therapist will guide her back to her feelings instead of diving into the process of solving the problem.

Women commonly ask why their partner says or does something. This is their attempt to find a solution to their problems. Rather than consider this question, a therapist will turn it around and say, "How does it make you feel when he says or does that?" By guiding her back to her feelings, the therapist will assist her in opening up to her feelings and releasing the stress of her life.

The guidelines of a Venus Talk help to ensure the same benefits a woman would get from regular therapy. Over time, she will get even more benefits, because she will begin to experience a new kind of intimacy with her partner that few couples ever experience. In addition to a greater understanding of how she feels, regular scheduled Venus Talks make him more sensitive to her needs and give him more awareness, motivation, and energy to support her.

How Venus Talks Work

A Venus Talk can only work when both the man and woman have the same goal. She can't expect him to apologize or promise to do something differently. She cannot expect him to prove his empathy in any way. Instead, she just shares, and he listens.

A Venus Talk is basically an FYIO message—
for your information only.
No action is required or expected.

If she talks about how much she has to do, she cannot expect him to offer his help. If he does, that is a bonus. She is only looking for him to listen. He may end up helping later, but her objective in talking is simply to talk about what is bothering her. The less she expects from him, the better she will feel, and the more he will do eventually.

When women expect more than what they are getting
from men, they will always get less.

If she says she has too much to do, she cannot expect him to offer to pick up the clothes at the cleaners, change the lightbulbs, review the credit card bills, or do a host of other chores. She is expecting him to listen to help her cope with stress so that her stress doesn't continue to overwhelm her.

A woman needs to remind a man each time they have a Venus Talk that he does not have to solve her problems. This is as new for him as it is for her. If she can't remember what she needs, she can't expect him to. By reminding him that he doesn't have to say anything or fix anything, she is also reminding herself that she is not expecting him to do anything.

A client of mine, who greatly resisted this process, tried it anyway. It seemed artificial and insincere to her. She didn't want to talk with someone who wasn't interested in what she had to say. In fact, her husband was not interested in what she talked about. She tried it, and she was amazed by how good she felt. She knew her partner was not that interested, but she had never been able to talk about anything without his interrupting her. Just that made it rewarding for her. Eventually, as he got better at it, he became interested in almost everything she said.

Just knowing that she will not be interrupted
can lower a woman's stress levels.

Some men need to feel successful at something before they get interested in doing it. Once a man discovers he can make his partner happy, the process of listening gives him the energy to stay interested. He may not care about everything she says, but he is interested in making her happy. New outfits, baby stories, office gossip, and wedding plans will never be as exciting to a man as they are to a woman.

Women Who Don't Talk Enough

Some women don't feel the need to share. They are too busy and don't want to be bothered. On the surface they appear to be from Mars, but inside they are still from Venus. In such cases women will still benefit from Venus Talks; they just don't know it until they try. These women are often with husbands or boyfriends who already talk too much. If she was to share, she would then have to listen to more of his problems. This would only raise her stress levels. It is fine for men to share feelings, but not after a Venus Talk. A general rule in gender communication at home is that men should never talk more than women. The last thing she needs to hear is his problems when she needs to talk or she is stressed.

A basic rule in gender communication is that
the man should never talk more than the woman.

Many women today don't even know that they have a need to express their emotions. They think confiding their problems to their partners is a relic of the 1950s. Women do not want to appear to be whiners or complainers. A woman's inability to feel this need to share feelings is the result of living in a stressful, testosterone-producing world. Although she doesn't feel the need, it is what she is missing the most. As she practices, during Venus Talks, she will begin to experience the many benefits of increasing oxytocin levels.

Scheduling Venus Talks

Instead of waiting for stress to build up, it is a good idea to schedule regular Venus Talks, just as you would a date or a therapy session. You should not wait until you have to talk. Just the pressure of having to get something out can restrict the production of oxytocin. Venus Talks are much more effective when they are planned, and a woman can look forward to that time.

A Venus Talk should ideally last about ten minutes and should be practiced at least three times a week. Of course at times of great stress she may need much longer to talk. At these times, she might consider talking first with a relationship coach or counselor so as not to burden her partner. During a Venus Talk, a woman needs to express how she feels about the stressful or difficult changes in her life, and her partner needs to listen and say occasionally, "Tell me more." He is not allowed to make comments, and she is not allowed to ask questions.

When the ten minutes are up, she thanks him, and he gives her a big hug. They generally do not talk about what she said, but if he wants to make a comment, he should wait for at least twelve hours. As my wife once said to me after a Venus Talk, "I need some time to bask in the sunshine of your love and understanding."

In the beginning, you may either feel you can't fill the entire ten minutes, or it may seem too short. Regardless, you should stick to the timing, and gradually you will develop the ability to turn your negative feelings on and off. Over the course of a few sessions, you will train your mind and body to begin producing more oxytocin within a short period of time.

Regularly scheduled Venus Talks will make other conversations much more stress-free. Venus Talks are a powerful way for both men and women to reduce stress levels. Just as a woman's oxytocin levels go up when she talks, a man's testosterone levels go up when he feels he is making a difference.

Using the Venus Talking Points

During your Venus Talks, I recommend using the Venus Talking Points listed below. This simple guide includes six questions for you to answer about your day, your week, your past, your childhood, or simply whatever comes into your mind.

Our subconscious mind knows what is bothering us and will release our stress when given an opportunity. All we need to do is ask the questions and talk about what comes up. By taking a brief time to explore and express what feelings arise with each question, a woman will experience rising oxytocin levels and consequently lower stress.

The Venus Talking Points

- ◆ What makes you feel frustrated, angry, or annoyed?
- ◆ What makes you feel disappointed, sad, or hurt?
- ◆ What makes you feel afraid, worried, or scared?
- ◆ What makes you feel sorry, embarrassed, or ashamed?

- What do you wish, want, or need?
- What do you appreciate, understand, or trust?

Take about ninety seconds to answer each of the six questions and share whatever comes up. If the question is about feelings of anger, but feelings of sadness arise, then talk about what makes you sad, but do take a moment to consider what makes you angry. Use this guide to assist you in looking within and sharing whatever you find.

The talks help to release women from the testosterone-oriented lock of setting and achieving goals. Not only is a woman letting go of expecting her partner to change as an outcome of her talking, but she is letting go of the idea that the Venus Talk should always be cathartic. Even if dwelling on a particular answer to a question feels good, it is better after a couple of minutes to move on to the next question. Limiting the time for each answer trains a woman's mind to explore feelings more efficiently and also helps her to move through her feelings more effectively.

Limiting the time of a Venus Talk trains the mind and body to release stress in a shorter period of time.

With regularly scheduled Venus Talks, a man sets up a new habit to help his partner lower her stress levels. And when a woman is happy, her partner is more likely to be. As a wonderful side effect, this process assists him in maintaining testosterone levels in her presence. Over time, his ability to listen will dramatically improve, and he will include her more in his thinking and decision-making process. The best attitude is to give up all expectations. Do not expect fireworks. If it happens occasionally, great.

Following the Basic Guidelines

Many women assume that their partners would not be interested in doing Venus Talks, but they are mistaken. When a man reads the basic guidelines and becomes aware of the many benefits for her, he is generally very happy to help. It is important for a woman to let him know each time that it was a big help. In the beginning, the process may seem a bit mechanical, but gradually it becomes very natural. It becomes a meaningful interaction that she will look forward to.

Venus Talks seem mechanical at first, but
eventually become natural and effortless.

Using the six Venus Talking Points make the process easier at the beginning. Once you get the hang of it, you may think that you don't need the points anymore. I recommend that you continue to use the points. The points are designed to direct the mind away from problem solving and keep her focused on her feelings. In addition, they gives the man something to do.

This is how a Venus Talk should go:

1. He reads the first question.
2. She begins to talk.
3. After about ninety seconds, he says "thank you," and then asks her the next question.
4. If she stops talking before ninety seconds are up, he can say, "Thank you, tell me more."
5. At no time is he to offer her advice, suggest something for her to say, apologize, or promise to do something.

6. At no point is he expected to solve her problem or answer her questions.

7. This is a time for her to lower stress and develop the habit of non-goal-oriented sharing.

8. When they are done, she should say something like, "Thanks for listening, it really helps. I feel much better."

9. Big hug.

Some women like and need this structure, while others are very happy just to talk about what is stressful or bothering them, as in the scenario at the start of this chapter. I would suggest using the Venus Talking Points many times before you decide if you want to use them again. These questions have proved immensely helpful for millions of people. I have taught this technique in a variety of ways for more than twenty-five years.

Use the Venus Talking Points many times
before you decide if you want to keep using them.

If you use the talking points enough, you internalize the point, and the questions might not be necessary for you. When you are first practicing the Venus Talks, it is easier if you don't focus on any feelings regarding your partner. There are plenty of other things to talk about. Eventually, as you get proficient, it is fine to talk about him if you wish to. By that time, you will both understand that you are just sharing your feelings and that you are not demanding more or asking him to change.

As women give up trying to change men, men begin to have more energy to remember their romantic feelings and provide that special kind of support. Having scheduled Venus Talks is a way to lower stress so that you can be more receptive and enjoy your relationship when your partner is romantic.

Why Venus Talks Work for Him

When a man doesn't have to fix anything, change in any way, or feel bad, then his brain is free to focus on one task—listening. When he does not have to defend himself or decide what he needs to do with the information she gives him, he is able to hear more of what she is trying to say. This kind of focus helps her to discover what she is feeling. As an author, I often write to discover what I know. As a speaker, I often speak to learn better what I already know. In a similar manner, women can talk to discover what they are feeling.

When a man listens, it helps
a woman to discover her feelings.

It can be very distracting for women to talk with a man, because every time she brings up a topic, she worries how to say it or how he will react. During a Venus Talk, she is free to say almost anything, and he will not get bent out of shape. It becomes easier for her to move through her negative feelings to discover the positive feelings that are always there.

Regular Venus Talks make communication easy. They take the pressure off a woman to get her partner's attention, and the pressure off him to solve her problems. Venus Talks free couples to understand each other and overcome the new burden of stress that we all carry.

Men and Feelings

At this point, you may be wondering whether a man needs to talk about his feelings. A man likes to share feelings, but he can do it after they have made love or while they are watching the sunset or the moonrise. Sharing feelings is a way for men to connect, but it is not the best way for him to release stress.

Sharing feelings is not the best way
for a man to release stress.

It can be useful for a man to explore and share his feelings to heal his past in therapy, or to help him go through a very stressful time. He will have the best results if he does so in a journal, with a relationship coach or counselor or with someone other than his romantic partner. She can support him by giving him lots of space and appreciating what he does.

When a man cares for the feelings of his romantic partner, his romantic attraction grows. When a woman becomes too involved in how her partner feels, she tends to become more maternal and goal-oriented, taking too much responsibility for him. This not only weakens him but places an additional burden on her.

Rather than relying on emotional support from his partner, a man can best cope with his stress by solving problems and being there for her. Having Venus Talks for her is particularly good for a man even when he is going through a stressful time. Focusing on her problems can be a significant relief for him. This is why men will often watch the news. As he focuses on the problems of others, he can temporarily forget his own.

Instead of having to deal with and feel responsible for all the stressors and problems in his life, he can do something concrete that will help his partner. By doing this one simple task of listening, he can give up having to do all those other things for a time. Helping her in this way actually supports him as well.

By taking the time to listen, a man can
temporarily give up his other pressures.

Ironically, as a man feels he doesn't have to do more to please his partner, he will begin to do more. A greater understanding of what she experiences stimulates him and creates extra energy to be more affectionate, plan fun and romance, and finish his chores around the house.

Following the guidelines of Venus Talk makes communication between Mars and Venus so much easier. A man doesn't have to understand her feelings and find a solution at the same time. This makes listening so much easier. On Mars, men display their caring by doing something or saying something to solve the problem. In a Venus Talk, listening is the only thing he does to solve the problem.

Remember, a man's capacity for empathy is not nearly as developed as it is in a woman. The emotional part of the brain is twice as big in a woman; the stress center in a man's brain, the amygdala, is twice as big, and is directly linked to his action centers. His testosterone-oriented nature seeks to solve problems right away. When he understands that listening can solve her biggest problem, which is to increase oxytocin levels, he can easily do it.

With practice, the empathetic part of his brain will begin to develop. This is the miracle of the brain. If we don't use it, we lose it. If we challenge our brains or repeat a behavior, new brain cells grow, and new neural pathways are formed. As a man practices Venus Talk with his partner, he will gradually grow in his ability to feel empathy and compassion. This new man brings hope for the future. He is not a man who has become like a woman, but a man who has learned to listen with his heart.

CHAPTER TEN

LOOKING FOR LOVE
IN ALL THE RIGHT PLACES

In order to make your relationship a sanctuary from the stress you encounter everywhere else in your life, you have to drop the expectation or hope that your partner will be perfect. Although it might seem unromantic not to expect perfection from your partner, the opposite is true. There is nothing more wonderful than to love someone completely for who that person is, flaws and all. Learning to feel and express real love is in many ways the reason we are here in this world.

Letting go of the notion that your partner should be the primary source of love in your life is one of the smartest decisions you will ever make. In this case, you are not settling for a relationship that doesn't give you everything you want and need; instead you are embracing and appreciating the support a relationship can provide. Recognizing the limitations of what anyone can give you is a realistic and healthy approach that almost all happily married couples learn to adopt in some way.

*Adjusting our expectations
does not mean we are settling for less.*

When we commit ourselves to getting the love and support we need in life without putting this burden solely on our romantic partner, we create a hormonal cascade that can bring back the romance again and again. Whenever you are feeling that you are not getting enough from your relationship, take a moment to remember the 90/10 principle. Take responsibility for elevating your meter and feeling good; then it will be easy for your partner to make you feel great.

There are many places a man and a woman can look to find the extra love and support they need to raise their happiness meter to 90 percent. By taking responsibility to nurture and be nurtured by other sources of love and support, you relieve your partner of this impossible burden.

*By finding support and love independent of our
partners, we relieve them of an impossible burden.*

These different sources of support are like love vitamins. The romantic love our partner gives us is just one vitamin. If we are deficient in that vitamin, taking it makes a huge difference in our health and well-being. If we are deficient in all our other vitamins, we will be too sick to benefit from the support our partner offers, no matter how much they give.

Instead of feeling deprived in your relationship, you can

appreciate what you have. This shift in perspective can change your life. For example, if your partner doesn't like to dance, then you can appreciate that you have friends who do. It is the basis of making all your dreams come true. The more you focus on having what you want and need, the more you will get. If you continue to focus on what you don't want, then that is all you see, and that is what you get.

Another unhealthy expectation comes from wanting your partner to be just like you. If that were true, there would never be any newness. Shared likes and preferences create comfort, but too much comfort creates boredom. The differences between a man and a woman create attraction and passion. Besides acknowledging and appreciating our differences, we need to also create some distance. To experience the excitement of coming together, you must also spend time apart.

> To experience the excitement of coming together,
> you must spend time apart.

You will deplete your energy supplies and increase the stress in your relationship if you expect your partner to be the primary source of your fulfillment. When you take responsibility for your life and your fulfillment, then and only then will you diminish the effects of stress on your relationship. This does not mean that your life or relationship will be perfect, but it does mean that you will be better equipped to balance the limitations of your relationship with the many blessings your partner and your life bring.

In this chapter, we will consider many sources of love and support that will relieve stress and enrich your life.

How to Fill Up Your Tank

Once you've accepted responsibility for 90 percent of your fulfillment, by treating yourself to oxytocin-producing activities, you are almost there, because following through will bring you so much pleasure. Though you might often feel that you run from crisis to crisis and that you do not have time to fit another thing into your overscheduled life, pursuing any one of the suggestions in the following pages will have such a positive effect, you will be inspired to do more. You have to try to achieve a balance in your life. When you take time for yourself and take care of yourself, you will be able to accomplish more and defuse the crippling effects of stress.

There are three areas in which to find stress-relieving support in your life:

- Fostering your inner life
- Building a network of support
- Living well

Considering different ways to enrich your life will open you up to experiencing a profound fulfillment that will keep stress at bay.

Fostering Your Inner Life

Unless you accept yourself and nurture the best in you, you will have trouble building a deep and lasting relationship with someone else. In the pages that follow, we will consider specific ways to foster a strong inner life that will make connecting with others less stressful and tumultuous.

To find sources of inner strength, look to:

- Yourself
- Spiritual and inspirational support
- Your priorities
- Individual therapy or life coaching

Look to Yourself

To accept the love of others, you need to love yourself first. Treating yourself with kindness, respect, and compassion is the foundation for feeling good. When you cannot generate a feeling of well-being and self-acceptance in yourself, it is unrealistic to expect your partner to make you feel good about yourself. His or her support will never be enough, because you need a healthy self-image before you can believe the support offered by someone else.

In the beginning of a relationship, just being with your new love makes you feel so good. You see yourself reflected in your lover's eyes. Once the newness wears off, you need to focus more on loving yourself.

One way to love yourself is to do things for yourself that you would do for someone else you love. Another is to treat your body with extra care. Eating delicious and healthy food is a way of loving yourself, as is getting enough exercise and sleep. Not letting others mistreat or walk over you will make you feel good about yourself. As you focus on finding ways to love yourself, you open the door for others to love you as well.

Look to Spiritual and Inspirational Support

Spiritual or inspirational support, so important in our lives, becomes even more significant when you are under extreme stress. If you do not have a relationship with a higher power or are not striving in some way to connect to a greater potential within yourself, you will be driven by an unrealistic expectation for your partner and yourself to be perfect. The unhealthy demand for perfection is a symptom of not accepting the need to connect with some form of a higher power, of not seeing your life in the grand scheme of things. In some cases, therapy or personal growth seminars can help meet this need, since such activities will assist you to discover and believe in your inner potential.

Look to Your Priorities

If you do not follow clear priorities to nurture and support yourself and your family first, it is very easy to feel that your partner is not making you a priority. Focus more on what is important, and give up trying to be everything for everyone. Do not try to accomplish all your goals tomorrow. Only when you have your priorities right can you be receptive to receiving more support from your relationship. Men and women have to make stress relief a priority every day.

Look to Individual Therapy or Life Coaching

If you have unresolved issues from childhood, or serious emotional problems, it is very important to handle these separately from your partner. Not only can individual therapy or life coaching be fulfilling and empowering, but it also releases the unhealthy desire for our partner to be a teacher, guide, and parent all wrapped up in one.

By having private sessions, you will have an opportunity to vent your thoughts and feelings as well as explore your goals and strategies without having to worry about hurting anyone or being held accountable for what you have said. So many relationships are ruined when people have no one else with whom to talk. Either they suppress themselves by not talking things out, or their negative thoughts and feelings can surface at the most inappropriate times.

Remember, it takes two to create a conflict, but only one to begin resolving the situation. When you resist, resent, or reject a situation, it not only takes a toll on you, but it inhibits the possibility of resolution and positive change. In many ways, the world is a mirror of our mood. If we let it bring us down for long, we lose touch with our inner ability to create change by inspiring others to be their best. And if we cannot change others, at least we can use challenging situations to bring out the best in ourselves. When you are more aware of how you are contributing to a problem, you can then make small adjustments in your attitude and behaviors that can make a huge difference in all your relationships at home and at work.

If you need to talk, and you don't know where to turn, you can get support at www.marsvenus.com. We provide online or phone coaching whenever you feel the need. Sometimes a person doesn't want to make the commitment to regular therapy but simply needs to talk with a trained relationship coach. A Mars Venus Relationship Coach is available for as long as you need and whenever. You can schedule a regular appointment or simply call at times of stress or confusion.

Building a Network of Support

Isolation is a major contributor to the rising stress everyone is experiencing. People are working so hard that they have less time to socialize. Families are scattered throughout the country, so the safety net of the extended family is out of reach for many. DVDs, TiVo, and Internet shopping make it possible for people to stay at home, reducing their interactions with others. BlackBerries, Trios, and cell phones may make people feel as if they are in touch, but much of our communication is only digital. Cyber-friendships and interactive sites can provide support, but it exists in the Ethernet. We also need personal interactions.

The fact is, going it alone doesn't reduce stress. While this is harder on women than men, men still need personal interactions and support. Isolation from the world can put an enormous amount of pressure on your partner. You need to balance your dependence on your partner for human contact by developing your relationships with others. You must look to:

- Family members
- Friends
- Work and coworkers
- Mentors
- Support groups
- Other couples

Look to Family Members

One of the biggest sources of stress today, particularly for women, is the fragmentation of the family. Family is certainly important for men, but much more so for women. Staying in touch and spending time with the family is nurturing to a woman's soul. If you neglect this need, you will expect your partner to fill in this gap.

Your parents provide a special kind of support that will keep you grounded in your past and history. This support creates a sense of belonging and security. Without this foundation, you can find yourself looking to your partner for parental support, or you can behave as if you are your partner's parent. Looking to your partner as a parental substitute can be nurturing in the beginning, but eventually making your partner your parent will end the romance and passion.

If you are looking for parental support and you can't get that support from your parents for whatever reason, then find a therapist. A therapist or relationship coach is a more appropriate way to nurture your needs and make up for what was missing in your childhood.

Look to Your Friendships

When you don't take time to create and nurture friendships, you expect your partner to fill this void. The need for friendships must be met; otherwise you will rely too heavily on your partner. Women expect their partners to be chatty like a girlfriend, and men expect their partners to be as easygoing or low-maintenance as their male friends. Many couples, who run out of passion, feel as if their partners are their best friend. They would do better to find a best friend outside the relationship. We can still be best friends, but a healthy distance can spark feelings of attraction and sustain them.

Look to Your Work and Coworkers

If you are lucky, what you do to make a living is also a passion. Even if your work is not that fulfilling, at least you have a source of connection in your colleagues, clients, and everyone else who works in your field. Join professional organizations and office teams and contribute to fund-raising events to expand your base of support.

If you do not work at an outside job, there is so much you can do to contribute to your community and various charities. You will be working with others for common goals to help the less fortunate, which will do a lot to raise oxytocin and testosterone.

When you do not have meaningful work in your life, you will expect your partner to make your life more meaningful. A romantic partner can never be a substitute for your need to make a difference in the world. It is very important to feel you are contributing in some way to the well-being of others. Such activities will make you feel connected and build your sense of self-worth. If you do not regularly experience being valued outside your home and family, you will become too dependent on your partner to make you feel good. Women begin to feel as if they don't matter to their partner, and men become temperamental.

Look to a Mentor

Find an older person whom you trust and respect to confide in and to give you advice. Whether a professional or social contact, your mentor has been through a lot, and you can benefit from his or her experience. Your mentor should be able to give you hard-won practical advice as well as a calm perspective on the vicissitudes of your life. Without a mentor in life, we tend to be too hard on ourselves for not having all the answers, or we regret that our partners are not wiser.

Look to Some Kind of Support Group

One of the most powerful hormone stimulators in our lives can be a support group with members of the same sex. Women's support groups have a tremendously positive effect on a woman's oxytocin levels through the tend-and-befriend path to stress reduction. Just being together raises women's oxytocin levels. Scheduling a couple of hours each week to share what is going on in your life with girlfriends makes a huge difference. It could be in a reading group or a weekly bridge game. It could be going with friends to an aerobics class and stopping for coffee after. These exchanges are important in filling up your tank.

Women today are missing the hormonal stimulation that comes when women share, communicate, commiserate, and cooperate in a context that is not work-oriented. Just talking about what is going on in your life without the intent to fix anyone or solve anything ends up being one of the most practical things you and your women friends can do. Just looking forward to your meetings will sustain higher oxytocin levels.

The work world often gives men this kind of support, but a men's support group can give a man the opportunity to express what's going on in his life without having to edit himself. Going out to the movies with friends, being on a sports team, or simply going to a sporting event with "the guys" can be testosterone-stimulating. Being with women or with his partner for a long time can actually lower a man's testosterone level. He can begin to feel tired in her presence, or feel as if he can't breathe freely around her. This is not her fault. It is simply that he is not getting enough time with his male friends.

This is particularly important when a man works in a female-dominated environment like fashion, publishing, schools, and hospitals. Surrounded by women, a man can easily become exhausted if he is not renewed through hanging out with other Martians some of the time.

Look to Other Couples

Spending time as a couple with other couples gives a great boost to your relationship. It has many benefits. It allows you to be in your partner's presence and see him or her through the eyes of others. This increases the feelings of newness.

When you spend time with other couples, you tell old stories or discuss what is going on in your life. You would normally never bring these things up, because your partner is familiar with the stories and your life. Since your friends have not yet heard all your stories or what is happening new in your life, a feeling of newness is stimulated in everyone.

Talking about current events, movies, and the arts with other couples will expand your perspective and interests. Hearing your partner express his opinions to others will help you to appreciate his perspective even more.

Talking with the same person over the years tends to bring out predictable responses. Conversation with others will evoke new opinions and ideas. Even though you are talking to another couple, the fresh perspectives you express are revealed to your partner as well.

Living Well

Once you have expanded the base of your contacts to fill up your tank without depending on your partner, you can look to the way you live your life. The more you have in your life that engages and fascinates you, the more interesting you will become. The more you fill yourself up with things that expand your mind and your heart, the more energy and enthusiasm you will have. Stress will not be able to distort your outlook or break your spirit. If you want to live a joyful life that won't be disrupted by tension and pressure, look to:

- What you eat, how you exercise, and how much you sleep
- Your schedule
- Rest, recreation, hobbies, and vacations
- Special community occasions
- Continuing education

- Unconditional support for children, the underprivileged, or a pet
- Books, movies, theater, art, and TV
- Outside help

Look to What You Eat, How You Exercise, and How Much You Sleep

Without a healthy diet or food plan, many people experience different degrees of mood swings, anxiety, and depression. Understanding what foods to eat to achieve optimal health can make a huge difference in how you deal with stress.

Just learning to omit certain foods can minimize fatigue and reduce stress in a few days. There are also certain brain minerals that can immediately boost healthy brain chemicals, like dopamine and serotonin, that make us feel good. My previous book, *The Mars and Venus Diet and Exercise Solution,* details a program to assure optimal health for men and women.

Eating right and taking some time to exercise each week will make a substantial difference in your self-esteem and well-being. Even moderate exercise a few hours a week can help you to feel good about yourself. In addition to fostering well-being, exercise first thing in the morning will help you to sleep better at night. You know how much better you feel after a good night's sleep.

For those who need a little extra support in exercising, I have a DVD of me doing a routine of Mars Venus Exercises. You can find out more about diet and this specially designed exercise program at www.marsvenus.com or in my Mars Venus Relationship Makeover Program.

In order to restore optimal hormone levels and for our bodies to recover from the stress of our days, we need to get at least eight hours of sleep a night. Those who do live longer and healthier.

With so much exposure to chemical toxins in the air, the water, our food supply, and our environment, we need to give our bodies a chance to cleanse themselves at the cellular level. When toxins are successfully released, your cells can receive not only more nutrients but more oxygen as well. This not only gives you more energy, but the increased oxygenation of cells can also eliminate many of the most threatening diseases.

Cleansing is one of the oldest healing practices in history. Every culture and religion includes some kind of cleansing or fasting process to be observed occasionally. The need for cleansing is even more important today, when we are exposed to so many more toxins.

The need for cleansing is more important today
because we are being exposed to so many more toxins.

When you take care of your physical needs and care for yourself in a nurturing manner, you will automatically begin to feel more positive about yourself and your life. You will feel like a winner, with plenty of love and energy to share. If you want to learn more about reducing stress and cellular cleansing, turn to appendix A, "Reducing Stress through Cellular Cleansing."

Look to Your Schedule

When you don't take time for yourself, you will often feel that your partner is not taking enough time for you. If you cannot first be there for yourself, don't expect anyone else to. Ideally, busy couples should sit together with a calendar to schedule time to spend together.

When special times are scheduled on the calendar, it helps a woman to remember she is not alone and gives her something to look forward to. For a man, scheduling is most important; otherwise he very easily overlooks taking time to enjoy his relationship. He gets too caught up in solving the problems of providing for his family, and forgets to take time to be with them. He doesn't realize how quickly time passes, and how much his presence is needed and appreciated.

Look to Rest, Recreation, Hobbies, and Vacations

When you don't take time for relaxation and recreation, you may unfairly expect your partner to entertain you or make life fun. When life becomes flat or boring, you blame your partner instead of taking time out for fun on your own. Whether fishing, biking, playing poker, or raising bees, men typically need some kind of regular hobby that helps them take their minds off work. Women need regular little vacations or getaways to escape all the things that remind her of everything she needs to do. Eating out is helpful for a woman, because she doesn't feel the pressure to prepare the menu, do the shopping, cook, and then clean up. Though these tasks can be a great source of fulfillment, she also needs a break.

Look to Special Community Occasions

Occasions like family get-togethers, reunions, birthdays, weddings, anniversary parties, religious or spiritual observances, and celebrations like parades, fairs, dances, and public concerts fulfill our need to feel special. We can also share our good feelings with so many others. Without these experiences on a regular basis, you will rely too much on your partner to make you feel special. You cannot expect romance to do it all.

Look to Continuing Your Education

A major source of newness in life is continuing to learn. Learning new things not only promotes the production of stress-reducing hormones but actually stimulates the growth of brain cells and new neural connections.

Taking a class at a local community college or spiritual community, or a personal growth seminar, can provide a lift to our energy levels.

Besides finding newness by learning new things, it can also be helpful for you to develop new skills. Taking a class to learn a new skill will definitely bring something engaging into your life. Take a cooking class, a dance class, a karate class, a poetry or memoir writing class, a painting or drawing class.

When you are studying something new, you are in the positive state of having beginner's awareness. One of the reasons young children have so much love, energy, and vitality is that everything is new to them. When you take classes and learn from others who have devoted themselves to a subject, a whole new world opens up to you. This more vulnerable state of mind opens your awareness to appreciate the wonders of life and your partner more. You will regard your partner with new eyes and see more qualities you can admire and love, just as you did at the beginning of your relationship.

Look to Unconditional Support for Children, the Underprivileged, or a Pet

We all have the need to give and receive unconditional love and support. When you give unconditionally, it affirms your inner abundance. Doing so will remind you that you have a place in this world, and you make a difference. Ultimately, we are here to serve each other in love and fairness. This truth is often lost, forgotten in the pressures of the real world. Your challenge in life is to remember this innocent vision of life and integrate it into the way you live to the best of your ability.

Giving unconditionally is most appropriate when you give to those who need us the most and have little to give back except love. By caring for children, a pet, the poor, or the disabled not only will you help those who can most appreciate what you have to offer, but you get to experience the joy of giving without strings.

One of the reasons a relationship is so wonderful in the beginning is that you give so generously. You are giving freely, because you assume that it will all come back. When you don't receive what you expect in return, you begin to hold back or resent your partner for giving less. At these times, the real source of your pain is that you have stopped giving of yourself unconditionally.

Our greatest pain is when we stop freely
giving of ourselves.

By intentionally giving to those who cannot give back, you remind yourself of the joy of unconditional giving. You return to your sense of fullness and are once again more willing to let your heart overflow into your relationship and life.

Look to Books, Movies, Theater, Art, and TV

A great source of newness and stimulation is reading, watching movies and TV, or going to the theater. Making sure you take the time to get the stimulation and entertainment you need will free you from expecting your partner to entertain you.

A good action or adventure movie can stimulate testosterone

production for a man, just as a romantic comedy or chick flick can do wonders to raise a woman's oxytocin level. Having a good book to cuddle up with can be a great stress reducer, engaging you in another world or introducing you to new ideas. Looking at art or a music or dance performance can elevate your spirits by reminding you of what we can accomplish.

Hearing the stories of others will increase your awareness of yourself and the story of your life. This will free you from making your romantic partner the center of your life by excluding other sources of love and support. In this sense, entertainment can remind you to look for love in all the right places.

Look to Outside Help to Relieve the Stress

With so much to do and so little time, it is unrealistic for couples to expect each other to maintain a home the way their parents did without extra help. Having more to do than we have the energy or time for creates extra stress for both women and men. He should not expect her to do it all. If he does not have the energy at the end of the day to fill in the gap, a couple should get more help. Without it, they will both be too stressed out to feel good.

Keep in mind that when women handled all the cooking and cleaning, they were not going to work every day. Just as a man needs a break at the end of his day, a woman needs time to rest as well. Hired help can make a big difference when couples are just too busy or overworked to do it all.

Today, the pace of life is such that women who are homemakers need help as well. Often, many hours a day are spent taking children to various activities. The "overscheduled child" is a reality today, and women spend a staggering number of hours chauffeuring their children from event to event. These women deserve help to allow them to carve out some time for themselves.

If women are to spend many hours outside the home earning money, a big portion of their earnings needs to be budgeted to hire a housecleaner or a laundry service. If a woman's primary job is to run the household, she probably needs help as well. Without this support, a woman easily feels overwhelmed and then exerts an unhealthy pressure for her partner to help. If he is already exhausted after his day at work, to expect more than he has the energy to give drives a wedge between them.

If you can't afford to have someone come in every other week to do the heavy cleaning, you should organize sharing the chores in a way that relieves the day-to-day stress about who does what and when.

You Have Everything You Need, and You Always Did

Looking for love in all the right places is one of the best strategies I know to help couples make their dreams come true. There is nothing more wonderful than feeling you have more to give instead of running on empty. But this strategy comes with a warning.

Though you get love and support from friends, you could potentially use your friendships against yourself and your relationship if you do not have the right attitude. In such situations, you turn the support you get from a friend against your partner. Here are a few examples of how you can misuse the support you get from outside relationships and increase the stress with your partner:

- ◆ "My friend accepts me just the way I am. Why can't you?"
- ◆ "Everyone at work thinks I am brilliant, but you constantly disagree with me."

- "It was a wonderful exhibition. I wish you had come so that we could have enjoyed it together."
- "Everyone in my support group understands me. Why can't you?"
- "I enjoy gardening so much. I wish you loved it as much as I do."
- "I know you don't like action movies, but Bill's wife goes with him."
- "Carol's husband is a good cook. I wish you would help out in the kitchen."
- "The farmer's market is such a wonderful community experience. If only you would share it with me. I don't like going alone."
- "I had such a good time at dancing class. I don't know why I even bother to learn. You just want to sit in front of the television."
- "What a beautiful sunset, and you haven't even noticed. You're too busy making calls."
- "Look at that loving couple. I remember when you used to hold me that way."

Each of these remarks focuses on what you are not getting from your partner, ignoring the support you do receive. Instead of feeling gratitude and fulfillment for what you get from the world, you can use it to underscore what you think you are missing. Instead of having more to bring home to your romantic partner, you have less. In some cases, the more you get from the world, the more you resent that your partner does not provide the same kind of support.

It is painful to feel that you are not getting what you deserve, but it feels just as bad to be treated as though you owe more. No one likes to feel in debt. Feelings of obligation may ruin friendships, but they kill romance.

Feelings of obligation may ruin friendships,
but they kill romance.

We all deserve so much more than we get. That is life. Your job is to open your heart to recognize where you can get the support you need. Life is a process of discovering that you have everything you need, and you always did. In this moment, you have just what you need to move in the direction of getting more of what you deserve. You limit yourself too much if you expect your partner to do it all.

Life is a process of discovering that you have
everything you need, and you always did.

Your happiness in life and love is a matter of what you choose to focus on and then create.

CREATING A LIFETIME OF LOVE

To create a lifetime of love, passion, and attraction, we must deal with stress first. Romance is not possible if you are tense, tired, or overwhelmed. Instead of focusing on creating romance, you need first to reduce the stress in your life.

Women today long for romance, because romance is the most powerful oxytocin producer. Throughout the world, as more women achieve financial independence, their romantic needs have dramatically increased. Successful women put a high premium on romance. The increased oxytocin produced by romance is a powerful antidote to the stress of working in a testosterone-oriented work world.

Even the most self-sufficient woman today will acknowledge her need to experience a man's romantic love. Compliments, affection, attention, courtesies, flowers, dates, presents, surprises, candle-lit dinners, and making love are as important as ever, if not a bigger priority.

As you have seen, a man can score big points with a woman by learning to do the little things that say "I love you," and occasionally creating a very romantic evening or getaway. Support like this will raise a woman's oxytocin levels and reduce her stress.

Instead of expecting a man to think of romance, a woman needs to remember that he is from Mars and tends to think in terms of projects with a clear beginning and end. Once he has succeeded in being romantic, he thinks he is done. To make sure your partner continues to meet your romantic needs, you must not expect him always to remember on his own. It certainly feels more romantic when he does it on his own, but if he doesn't, then it is up to you to remind him.

One of the biggest obstacles to lasting romance is that women feel a variety of wants, wishes, and needs, but do not express them. Men need to hear clear, friendly, and short requests. In the beginning, a man does not need to hear his partner's needs and requests, because his goal is for her to know that he is there for her. He is constantly thinking of ways to communicate that message. Later in the relationship, he assumes she must be getting what she wants if she is not asking for more. On the other hand, if she complains he is not doing enough, he does not feel like being romantic. On Mars, it is almost impossible to feel romantic when someone is complaining that you are not enough. Remember, success and not failure stimulates testosterone.

In the beginning women don't need to ask,
because men are so eager to please.

Asking for what she wants is always hard on Venus, but asking for romance can be even more difficult. It is a new skill, but it can be learned. When she feels ignored and less important than her partner's work, it is harder for her to ask for what she wants, particularly because she is asking for romance. The only way some women know how to ask for more is to complain. Unfortunately, this approach is counterproductive and puts a damper on the romance. Most women who do complain already sense it will not work, but they don't know what else to do. Now they can discover a way that works.

Ways to Ask for Romance

Remember, it is important to approach a man in a positive and appreciative way. Here are some examples of how women can ask for romance:

- "There is a new play in town. I would love it if you planned a date for us to see it. I feel like going out—just the two of us."
- "There is a concert coming up, and I got tickets. Would you put it on your calendar and take me, please?"
- "I have been invited to a party by my friend Carol. Would you take me, please? I know you don't like parties much, but it would feel so good if you were there."
- "I had a big day today, and I'd like to celebrate. Would you make reservations and take us out to dinner?"
- "I was reading about this beach near Muir Woods. Let's hang out there on Saturday. I will make a picnic. Would you drive?"
- "I got my hair cut today. I like it a lot. I know haircuts are not that important to you, but it feels really good when you notice and say something. Next time, would you say how great I look?"
- "When you see me all dressed up for the party, would you let me know that you think I look beautiful? I know you do, but it just feels good to hear you say so."

- "I bought these two little candles. I thought it would be fun to light one if I was in the mood for making love, or you could light it when you are in the mood, and I would light the other to let you know when I am ready."

- "Would you please take care of the dishes tonight? I can't do another thing, and I'd like to take a bubble bath."

- "I am planning to go to an exhibit at the Historical Society. I'd be happy to go alone, but I would love it much more if you would take me."

- "Sometimes I miss hearing you say you love me. I know you do, but it is nice to hear you say it."

- "Let's slow down. I really like this."

As you can see, each of these requests is direct, brief, and positive. There is no list of complaints to justify asking for his support. The fewer words she uses, the easier it will be for him to take action and give her the support she wants.

Love Conquers All

To keep love and passion alive, it takes much more than trying to repeat what happened so easily in the past. You must learn new skills and approaches to reduce the high level of stress in your life, some of which results from changing male and female roles.

Unless we adapt by applying the strategies discussed in *Why Mars and Venus Collide,* divorce and sickness could well be our destiny. It is not enough simply to react to life's changes. You must take hold of your life and repeatedly and dynamically correct the direction you are being taken. You have to work with your partner and your biology to reduce the stress in your lives.

You cannot simply behave and respond however you happen to

feel that day. To love someone, you must deliberately and wisely choose what you do and how you respond. When you make your partner more important than how you feel, you will feel more love and connection.

Love is more than just a feeling. Love is an overriding attitude that manages and organizes what we choose to do and how we choose to respond in the service of those for whom we care. Ultimately, we should not give love to get what we need. Instead, love is its own reward.

Inner Fulfillment

If you can learn to lower your stress levels by experiencing an inner fulfillment independent of your partner, you can then bring back the wonderful feelings you experienced in the beginning of your relationship. By applying the insights found in these pages, you can overcome the stress that confronts you and your partner each day. With new strategies based on our hormonal differences, we can overcome the increasing tendency for men to become more passive and women to become more demanding.

> Together we can overcome the tendency for men
> to become more passive and women
> to become more demanding.

By learning these new methods of coping with stress, you will prepare the foundation to sustain or awaken your romantic behaviors and responses once again. During this process, it is vital to remember that these caring and trusting behaviors are automatic in a new relationship but change as time sets in. Expecting automatic romance in long-lasting relationships will set you up for failure and rejection. Expecting your partner to repeat those behaviors is especially unrealistic if he is under the influence of rising stress levels.

The irony in relationships is that in the beginning we instinctively do the very things that stimulate high levels of testosterone in men and oxytocin in women, but as time passes, we resist doing the very things that will make us feel great.

Study the following chart to remind yourself of how our behavior changes with our partners:

MARS IN THE BEGINNING AND LATER:	VENUS IN THE BEGINNING AND LATER:
He plans dates / He waits to find out what she wants to do.	She is delighted by his plans / She seeks to improve on his plans.
He is interested in what she did that day / Assuming he already knows about her day, he just says hi and reads the news.	She talks about the problems of her day / She expresses feelings or complaints about him or their relationship.
He gives her compliments and makes reassuring gestures that she is loved / Assuming that she already knows he loves her, he stops.	She shares her concerns and worries / Knowing that he will try to solve things, she shares her concerns and worries about him.
He shares his hopes, plans, and dreams / To avoid criticism or correction, he keeps them hidden.	She admires his ideas and plans / In an attempt to help him, she points out what is wrong or missing in his plans.
He does a variety of little things to make her happy / He just focuses on the big things like making a living and providing for her.	She enjoys doing many things for him / She feels burdened by having to do so much.

MARS IN THE BEGINNING AND LATER:	VENUS IN THE BEGINNING AND LATER:
He takes plenty of time in sex so that her needs are met / He assumes she doesn't need or want more time.	She enjoys having sex / She feels too tired, overwhelmed, or stressed to have sex.
He is interested in her feedback / He backs off because he has heard it before.	She appreciates the way he does things / She offers unsolicited help and advice.
He plans dates, getaways, and vacations / He waits to find out what she wants to do, because she seems to have so many more requirements.	She enjoys taking time for fun things / She resists taking time off, because she has so much to do.
He starts out giving her lots of support and attention / As she gives him so much in return, he assumes that she is getting enough and stops.	She freely gives and receives in the beginning / When she is not getting as much, she gives more instead of asking for more or taking time for herself.
He takes risks and plans new things / He becomes more sedentary and does less, or repeats the same things.	She appreciates his passion / She puts a damper on that passion by pointing out his mistakes in the past.
He showers her with love and affection / He becomes engrossed in his work.	She happily gives her love and support without strings / When her support is not reciprocated, she feels taken for granted and resentful.
He brings her flowers / Since he is doing the big stuff like providing and being faithful, he assumes he doesn't need to do the little stuff.	She accepts him just the way he is / She expects him to know and do certain things. If she has to ask, it doesn't count.

When we are in the honeymoon stage, it is easy to be impervious to the many stresses in our lives. Once the newness of love has passed, we inevitably become vulnerable to that massive stress. If you can just remember that your partner's loving behavior was just a glimpse of how you can be together, it creates hope instead of despair. Such a vision should motivate you to take responsibility for your happiness without blaming your partner. This attitude will free you to give your love unconditionally.

Once the newness of love has passed, we gradually
become vulnerable to the massive stress in our lives.

A woman's greatest attribute is the ability to see the potential of something or someone. When she is feeling good, she can see all that is good in someone, but when she is feeling stressed, she only sees what has gone wrong or could go wrong.

When a woman falls in love, she is actually in love to some degree with a man's potential. If she becomes stressed over time, she can lose this vision and become hopeless. Without hope, both men and women lose touch with their ability to love freely.

Many women give up in their relationships, because they don't get back what their partners used to provide in the beginning. When the warm affection and interest that were so intense in the beginning dissipate, these women eventually pull back from giving of themselves.

Instead of resenting our partners, we must focus on lowering stress and feeling good again. As we begin to feel better, it becomes easier to assist our partner in overcoming the stress in his or her life. Sometimes all it takes for a man to feel better and to give more in a relationship is to feel that he could easily make his partner happier. When all he needs to do is top her off, he is suddenly much more available.

Doing What Works

If a man's testosterone is depleted, he feels too stressed to plan a date. He just does not feel like it. He does not realize that if he planned a date, much of his stress would go away. Planning dates will actually bring his testosterone level up again.

At work, a man doesn't think twice about doing things that he doesn't feel like doing. He does them because it is necessary to get the job done. His thought process is as follows: "I don't want to do it, but if it is necessary, then I am happy to do it." He can apply this approach to his relationship once he becomes aware of what is necessary. If he wants to keep the passion and attraction alive, he needs to do certain things even if he doesn't feel it.

To keep the passion alive, we must do what works
even if we don't feel like it.

With depleted oxytocin, a woman often feels too overwhelmed to go out on a date. If, however, she allows a man to plan it for her, even if the date is not exactly what she would have wanted to do, she will find that she begins to relax and be happy. When she allows him to take care of her, her stress is reduced, and she begins to smile again. She may not completely like the movie or restaurant, but she will appreciate his taking the initiative to make the plan and take care of her needs.

Saying Good-Bye to Romance

Statistics show that men after a divorce get married again within three years, but women take an average of nine years to remarry. This statistic just includes the women who get married again. Many more women than men just don't bother. They feel in a variety of ways that marriage is more trouble than it is worth. If a woman is financially independent, she is more unlikely to remarry. Instead, many women choose to live alone. In some cases, they are happier than before, but they still may be missing an opportunity for more in their lives.

These women mistakenly think the sole reason they are happier is that they don't have to bother with a passive partner who resists giving to them. But the real reason such a woman is happier is that she has given up expecting a man to make her happy and has finally taken responsibility for her own happiness. With these new insights, instead of getting a divorce to discover this inner ability, a woman can stay married and get the added bonus of a partner who is not only enriched by her fulfillment but rejoices in her happiness.

Divorced women are often happier,
because they have finally taken responsibility
for their own happiness.

Women who live alone and are happy have made an important adjustment. They have released the expectation that a man is needed to make them happy. The problem with this is that they have closed a door to letting a romantic partner take them from happy to happier, from feeling good to feeling great.

Realizing What Is Most Important

When someone dies unexpectedly, a common source of pain is the regret of not having let that person know how much we cared for him. It is as if we suddenly wake up and realize what is most important in life.

No one on his deathbed thinks much about his business mistakes. Instead, we reflect on the quality of our close relationships. Our greatest joy and sorrow comes from the experiences and decisions we make involving our intimate relationships.

A telling symptom of increased stress is our loss of perspective on what is most important in life. Creating time to love our partner and family is one of the greatest luxuries in life, and yet we often do not realize this until it is too late, and the opportunity is gone.

A telling symptom of increased stress is our loss of
perspective on what is most important in life.

Repeatedly, I hear the same story from heart disease and cancer survivors. They wake up and realize that their priorities in life were wrong. They made money, success, and perfection more important than simply loving the people close to them and enjoying more of what life brought them every day. Their demands on themselves diminish when they can appreciate just being alive.

We want to avoid waiting until the end of our lives to learn this lesson. If we begin to conquer the debilitating effects of stress today, we can dispel the illusion that we don't have the time or energy to love and cherish the people who are most important to us.

Women love to care for someone. When stress takes hold, a woman forgets she is doing what she loves to do, what nourishes her soul. Instead of freely giving, she may resent doing the things she used to love doing.

Men love to give in their way. Men endure the hardships and sacrifices required to succeed in the work world so that they can provide the needed support for their loved ones. Under the grip of stress, a man forgets the real reason he is working so hard. Without a partner or a family to care for, his life is empty. To protect and serve his wife and family gives his life meaning and purpose.

Just as a woman's role in life has expanded to being a partner with her spouse in the role of financially providing, a man's role has expanded beyond being a sole provider. Now he must also provide a new measure of emotional support to help his wife cope with new stresses in her life.

The Many Mysteries of the Opposite Sex

Understanding the differences in our hormones and the anatomy of our brains provides us with insights to help explain the many mysteries of the opposite sex. It may take a lifetime for us to understand each other fully, but the insights and techniques offered in *Why Mars and Venus Collide* can bring us much closer. Many things that didn't make sense begin to fall into place. That understanding can enrich our lives together.

What used to be annoying can become humorous. What used to hurt our feelings is no longer taken the wrong way. Where once we felt frustrated or helpless in our attempts to communicate our love as well as our needs, there is a new glimmer of hope for the future.

Mars and Venus do not have to collide. Together they can conquer stress by creating a lifetime of love.

Sharing Your Heart with Others

Thank you for making relationships and love a priority in your life. I hope that now you have a greater awareness of why Mars and Venus collide, and as a result you begin to create more love in your life. You certainly deserve it, and so does everyone else. I feel honored to share my heart with you and hope that you will continue to share your heart with others.

I invite you to join with me in helping others experience this exciting new information. So many families can be saved; so many hearts can be healed. Share this book with your family, friends, and children, not just when they are distressed and confused but also before the collisions occur. Creating a lifetime of love is our common challenge, and together, through sharing our hearts, we can make our dreams come true.

SOURCES

The scientific material found in chapters 2 and 3 is commonly accepted by scientists and medical doctors. These are some online references to give an accessible, and not too technical, overview.

On Brain Differences

Baron-Cohen, Simon. "They Just Can't Help It." *Guardian Unlimited,* April 17, 2003. http://education.guardian.co.uk/higher/research/story/0,,938022,00.html.

Hamann, Stephan. "Sex Differences in the Responses of the Human Amygdala." *Neuroscientist* 11, no. 4 (2005): 288–93. http://nro.sagepub.com/cgi/content/abstract/11/4/288.

"How Brain Gives Special Resonance to Emotional Memories." Adapted from a Duke University press release. *Science Daily,* June 10, 2004. http://www.sciencedaily.com/releases/2004/06/040610081107.htm.

"Intelligence in Men and Women Is a Gray and White Matter." *Today@UCI* (University of California, Irvine), January 20, 2005. http://today.uci.edu/news/release_detail.asp?key=1261.

Kastleman, Mark. "The Difference between the Male and Female Brain." SENS Self-Esteem Net. http://www.youareunique.co.uk/PgenderbrainII.htm.

"Male/Female Brain Differences." October 25, 2006. http://www.medicaleducationonline.org/index.php?option=com_content&task=view&id=46&Itemid=69.

"The Mismeasure of Woman." *Economist*, August 3, 2006. http://www.economist.com/research/articlesBySubject/displaystory.cfm?subjectid=348945&story_id=E1_SNQVJQJ.

Sabbatini, Renato. "Are There Differences between the Brains of Males and Females?" web.archieve.org/web/20041214165825/http://www.cerebromente.org.

Thornton, Jim. "Why the Female Brain Is Like a Swiss Army Knife." January 3, 1999. http://www.usaweekend.com/99_issues/990103/990103armyknife.html.

"Women Have Better Emotional Memory." Associated Press, July 22, 2002. http://www.usatoday.com/news/nation/2002-07-22-memory_x.htm.

On Testosterone

Girdler, Susan S., Larry D. Jammer, and David Shapiro. "Hostility, Testosterone, and Vascular Reactivity to Stress." *International Journal of Behavioral Medicine* 4, no. 3 (1997): 242–63.

Mason, Betsy. "Married Men Have Less Testosterone." *New Scientist*, May 22, 2002. http://www.newscientist.com/article/dn2310-married-men-have-less-testosterone.html.

Mitchell, Natasha. "Testosterone, The Many Gendered Hormone." http://www.abc.net.au/science/slab/testost/story.htm.

"Testosterone Background." http://www.seekwellness.com/andro pause/testosterone.htm.

"Testosterone Tumbling in American Males." October 27, 2006. http://health.yahoo.com/news/168226.

On Oxytocin

Barker, Susan E. "Cuddle Hormone: Research Links Oxytocin and Socio-sexual Behaviors." http://www.oxytocin.org/cuddle-hormone/index.html.

Foreman, Judy. "Women and Stress." August 13, 2002. http:// www.myhealthsense.com/F020813_womenStress.html.

"Oxytocin." http://encyclopedia.thefreedictionary.com/oxytocin.

Russo, Jennifer. "Womenkind: The Stress Friendly Species." http:// www.ivillage.co.uk/workcareer/survive/stress/articles/0,,156473 _162212,00.html.

Turner, R. A., M. Altemus, T. Enos, B. Cooper, and T. McGuiness. "Preliminary Research on Plasma Oxytocin in Normal Cycling Women: Investigating Emotion and Interpersonal Distress." *Psychiatry* 62, no. 2 (Summer 1999): 97–113. Also on http:// www.oxytocin.org/oxy/oxywomen.html.

Uvnas-Moberg, K. "Oxytocin May Mediate the Benefits of Positive Social Interaction and Emotions." *Psychoneuroendocrinology* 23, no. 8 (November 1998): 809–35. Also on http://www.oxy tocin.org/oxy/love.html.

On Stress

Eller, Daryn. "Stress and Gender." November 6, 2000. http:// women.webmd.com/features/stress-gender-feature.

"Cortisol." http://www.advance-health.com/cortisol.html.

"Cortisol & Weight Gain." http://annecollins.com/weight-control/cortisol-weight-gain.htm.

McCarthy, Lauren A. "Evolutionary and Biochemical Explanations for a Unique Female Stress Response: Tend-and-Befriend." http://www.personalityresearch.org/papers/mccarthy.html.

Neimark, Neil F. "The Fight or Flight Response." http://www.thebodysoulconnection.com/EducationCenter/fight.html.

Stoppler, Melissa Conrad. "Stress, Hormones and Weight Gain." http://www.medicinenet.com/script/main/art.asp?articlekey=53304.

"Stress, Cortisol and Weight Gain: Is Stress Sabotaging Your Weight and Health?" http://www.fitwoman.com/fitbriefings/stress.shtml.

"The Stress System: Adrenaline and Cortisol." http://en.wikibooks.org/wiki/Demystifying_Depression/The_Stress_System.

"Why Men and Women Handle Stress Differently." http://women.webmd.com/features/stress-women-men-cope.

REDUCING STRESS THROUGH CELLULAR CLEANSING

Repeatedly, I have witnessed the many miracles of cellular cleansing with thousands of people, both adults and children. Within seven days, blood sugar levels are balanced and food cravings are gone, blood pressure is normalized as stress levels drop, four to eight pounds of extra weight are released, bone mass begins to increase, and the needs for antidepressants and ADD drugs are replaced by sound sleep, positive moods, and abounding energy. Mars Venus cleansing coaches are available for free to assist, support, educate, and motivate you to follow a healthy nutritional program to balance hormones and stimulate healthy brain chemicals on a daily basis. Just as we need good relationship skills for stimulating healthy hormones and brain chemicals to lower stress, we also need to eat nutritious foods and take healthy supplements.

Relationship skills and behaviors can only stimulate the body to make healthy hormones and brain chemicals if the raw materials are available. If you are living on junk food, it will be much harder to get the results you deserve, no matter how many times you read this book. With the free assistance of a Mars Venus cleansing coach, you can most effectively support your relationships by taking some time to cleanse your body as well. You can refer to my Web site www.MarsVenus.com to get this additional support, or simply call 1-877-380-3053. It can be very powerful to let go of limiting and sometimes toxic beliefs and attitudes while also cleansing your body at the same time. I invite you to join our Mars Venus Wellness Community and after a few cleanses learn to coach others in the same process.

Relationship skills and behaviors can only stimulate
the body to make healthy hormones and brain
chemicals if the raw materials are also available.

Everyone knows, and no one disputes, that we live in a world filled with toxic chemicals that can increase our stress levels and cause a host of diseases. More importantly, these toxins and chemicals interfere with your body's natural ability to heal disease and cope effectively with stress. For some body types the gradual accumulation of toxins means increasing obesity, cancer, and heart disease, while for others it means osteoporosis, sleeplessness, and anxiety disorders. It would be naive to think that this stress doesn't take a toll on our relationships as well. Just as we need to let go of old roles and strategies for relating that don't work anymore, we also need to assist our bodies in letting go of toxins that we have accumulated throughout our lives. When we regularly cleanse our cells, then they can most effectively absorb the nutrition we require from the food we eat. Just as our cars get dirty and need to be cleaned on a regular basis, so do our bodies. It is not enough just to eat good foods; we need to assist the body in cleaning out toxic wastes and acids that prevent our cells from coping with stress to produce an abundance of energy.

It is exciting for me to share with you these natural solutions for healthy living and loving. It has taken a team of dedicated health, happiness, and relationship teachers, writers, coaches, researchers, therapists, doctors, nurses, patients, and seminar participants over thirty years to refine and develop the many resources available at www.MarsVenus.com. Much of this work is done today through special gatherings and seminars at the Mars Venus Wellness Center in northern California. For information on how you can attend a Mars Venus Wellness Retreat or Seminar taught by me or one of my trainers, call 1-877-JOHNGRAY (1-877-564-6472).

Everyone knows that medical drugs have dangerous side effects and should only be used when diet and exercise have failed. While most doctors are trained in treating disease, they know very little about creating health. In my weekly Internet TV show at www.MarsVenusWellness.com, I explore in great depth the principles of health for both men and women. The Mars Venus Wellness Solution reveals the secrets of restoring health without the need for drugs. In addition you will find a variety of gender-specific recipes and premixed healthy fast food formulas to support both men and women in getting the necessary nutrients to produce healthy brain chemicals and lower stress levels. The Mars Venus Wellness products are not only good for you but taste great as well.

In addition, the MarsVenus seven-day cleanse not only improves brain function and health but people who are overweight begin to lose extra pounds very quickly. The average weight loss for overweight people going through the cleanse at my ranch is eight pounds in a week. People who do not need to lose weight do not lose weight.

To receive a special free e-book containing this all-natural protocol for cellular cleansing of the whole body write to JG@Mars Venus.com

I hope you share my enthusiasm and begin to share these many resources with everyone you know. Together we can create a better world, one relationship at a time.

CREATING THE BRAIN CHEMICALS OF HEALTH, HAPPINESS, AND ROMANCE

Women's brains are much more affected by stress than those of men. With increased blood flow in the emotional parts of the brain, a woman is required to make more serotonin than a man to cope effectively with stress. Making more serotonin helps relax her brain and remind her of all that she has to be grateful for. By cleansing and supplementing her food plan with easy-to-digest proteins, omega-3 fatty acids, B vitamins, and lithium orotate, a woman can make an abundance of serotonin.

Serotonin is linked to optimism, comfort, and contentment: just what she needs to counteract the distress of increasing stress or danger. Men also require serotonin to cope with stress, but with so much more activity in the emotional part of the brain, women use up their serotonin supplies much faster than men. In addition, men store 50 percent more serotonin for emergencies and make it 50 percent more efficiently. This difference probably evolved to support men to cope effectively with the dangerous tasks they would undertake to protect their families. Today, women are taking on jobs that are just as stressful as those of men, but their brains don't make serotonin as efficiently. This helps to explain why women are so stressed today. This insight helps men be more motivated to help women solve this problem.

By stimulating more serotonin in her brain, a woman can cope more effectively with stress. Today billions of dollars are spent on drugs to assist women in increasing the effectiveness of serotonin levels to assist them in coping with the effects of depression and anxiety. Even the most conservative estimates indicate that women rely on at least twice as many antidepressants as men. My calculations indicate that it is more like ten times as many. While these antidepressants are a blessing to millions of women, they do not decrease the effects of stress. One of the many side effects of antidepressants is increased cortisol in the body. Cortisol is the stress hormone. When it goes up, our energy levels begin to decline. She may feel better on antidepressants, but her stress levels go up instead of down.

Antidepressants increase stress levels in the body.

The natural production of serotonin decreases stress levels in the body, but serotonin drugs actually increase cortisol levels. When a woman begins the use of an "SSRI" (selective serotonin reuptake inhibitor) antidepressant, her cortisol levels immediately double. As a result, many women eventually gain weight and experience less energy production. Other women who don't gain weight begin to crave sweets and simple carbohydrates for energy, and thus increase their risk of bone loss and osteoporosis. The by-product of excess sugar consumption is lactic acid, and this leaches the bones of calcium. Consuming extra calcium will not solve the problem of bone loss if women continue to eat excess carbohydrates and sustain higher cortisol levels. You can learn more about natural ways to create more serotonin in my book *The Mars and Venus Diet and Exercise Solution*. To receive a special free e-book containing an all-natural protocol for going off antidepressants or for children with ADD or ADHD write to JG@MarsVenus.com.

MARS VENUS COACHING AND COUNSELING

Sometimes there is just too much stress for dating or married couples to work through their problems on their own. No matter what one partner says, it just makes matters worse. When communication stops, it can be very helpful to get counseling or call a Mars Venus relationship coach. They are trained in the Mars Venus principles and can assist you in reducing stress levels by guiding you through Venus Talks. They can also help you find the answers you are looking for. It is not necessary for both partners to call. All it takes is one person to change his or her approach, and the dynamics in a relationship will change. By lowering your own stress levels, you will gain the ability to bring out the best in your partner as well as in yourself.

All it takes is one person to change his or her approach,
and the dynamics in a relationship will change.

Venus Talks and other emotional resolution processes can be helpful for men, just as they are for women. The big difference between men and women is that a cooperative male partner can be there for his female partner, but it is not recommended for a woman to be there for her male partner in this way. When women listen too much to a man's emotions and problems, they become more maternal, and this can reduce their feelings of sexual attraction for him. When a man needs emotional support to release his stresses, it is best to get the help of a counselor or coach.

A Mars Venus counselor or coach can help bring out our best side when our partners can't. Coaches help to remind us of who we are and what our options are. So many times stress will restrict our vision of possibilities. When we are upset, we are missing the bigger picture. Talking with someone who is not directly involved frees us to stand back and see the situation differently.

The extra benefit of phone coaching is convenience. You can be completely private, you don't even have to leave your home, and you don't have to make a commitment to long-term therapy. You can get quick help when you need it. It is even more economical. You can keep the same coach over a period of time, or you can change as often as you like. Each coach is trained in the Mars Venus principles, but sometimes you will have a favorite coach, whom you can easily request.

People commonly make the mistake of thinking they should be able to resolve relationship issues on their own. This is because we think the problem is always our partner; we conclude that this is either the wrong person for us, or that our partner is unwilling to change and get help. This is our biggest mistake. This attitude is not only arrogant but makes you a victim, stuck in a situation that can only get worse.

It takes two to create a conflict,
but only one to begin resolving the situation.

Having a coach listen to your feelings can help stimulate oxytocin for a woman and testosterone for a man. Having someone understand a woman's point of view will help stimulate the production of oxytocin, while having someone appreciate a man's efforts and assist him in problem solving will help stimulate the production of testosterone. Mars Venus coaches are trained to give gender-specific support, which many other counselors and coaches know very little about.

By getting help, you are affirming that you are not a victim of your partner or of the world. By taking a step to explore how you can make things better, you are immediately changing the dynamic of your relationships. You will discover how you may be making things worse, and how you can make things better. With new knowledge and insight, you can quickly move beyond feeling like a victim to instead getting more of what you want, need, and deserve. If you have the need to talk or you need answers to your questions, call a Mars Venus coach at 1-888-MARSVENUS (1-888-627-7836).

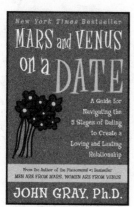
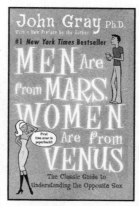

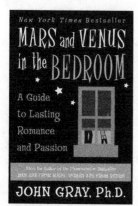
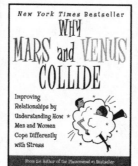

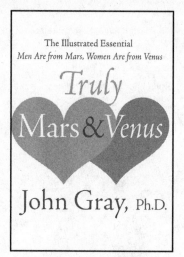

**10TH ANNIVERSARY
ILLUSTRATED EDITION**
Hardcover 978-0-06-008565-0

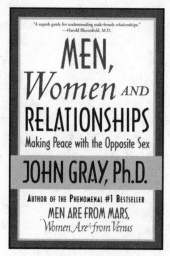

Paperback 978-0-06-050786-2

**Also available on Audio CD:
Mars & Venus in the Workplace**
Audio CD 978-0-06-123205-3

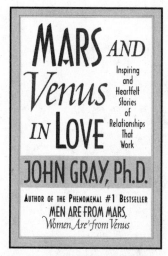

Paperback 978-0-06-050578-3

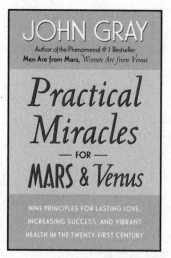

Paperback 978-0-06-093730-0
Audio CD 978-0-694-52371-9

Paperback 978-0-06-093099-8

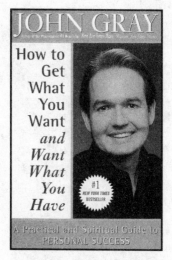

Paperback 978-0-06-093215-2
Large Print 978-0-06-093307-4

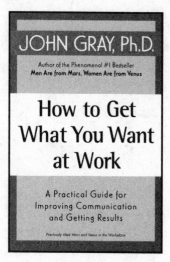

Paperback 978-0-06-095763-6

MarsVenusDating.com

• Join a growing community of like-minded singles. Membership is free.
• Get helpful tips and suggestions as you build your online profile.
• Benefit from our intuitive software that alerts you when you might be sending the wrong message to a potential match.

Join MarsVenusDating.com for free.

MarsVenusWellness.com

Tune in to Dr. John Gray's weekly internet radio and television show. Each week Dr. Gray explains how to apply his Relationships and Health concepts in two separate shows.

Relationships—*Men Are from Mars, Women are from Venus* comes alive as Dr. Gray offers insights that help reduce stress while nurturing long and happy relationships.

Health—Mars Venus Health provides a gender specific understanding of men's and women's unique needs for creating optimal health, hormonal balance, and optimal brain chemistry. Discover the secrets of health they don't teach in medical school. Learn how cleansing and the right nutrition for you can support your body's ability to effectively manage stress. Make small but significant changes in your lifestyle to create and maintain lasting mental focus, steady mood, and abundant energy.

For inspiring examples, important information, helpful tips, recipes, menus, and newsletters, we invite you to visit MarsVenusWellness.com. Increase your awareness for better choices!

Join the Mars Venus Global Wellness Community and receive weekly insight and inspiration for creating a lifetime of love and lasting health.

MarsVenusCoaching.com

Learn how to become a Mars Venus Relationship Coach. Join the global Mars Venus Coaching Team and:
• Help others achieve their relationship goals.
• Enjoy a flexible lifestyle.
• Have the support of a recognized global brand.
• Gain financial freedom doing what you love to do.

Contact www.marsvenuscoaching.com to learn more about this franchise opportunity.

Shop Online at the Mars Venus Store

At the Mars Venus Store at MarsVenus.com you can purchase a variety of books, audio and video programs, CDs and DVDs for all ages and stages of relationships.

Bestselling cassettes or CDs include:
• The Secrets of Successful Relationships (12-pack)
• Personal Success (12-pack)

Bestselling videos or DVDs include:
• Mars and Venus Together Forever (2-pack)
• Mars and Venus On a Date (2-pack)
• Mars and Venus Starting Over (2-pack)
• Children Are from Heaven (6-pack Parenting Guide)

The bestselling Mars and Venus Wellness Solution includes a gender specific nutritional program for health, happiness, and lasting health:
• Mars and Venus Super Cleanse (15 servings)
• Mars and Venus Super Minerals (30 servings)
• Mars and Venus Super Foods Shake (15 servings)

This wellness program is easy to use and immediately effective, and it tastes delicious. It can provide immediate relief from stress through the many benefits of optimal brain function and hormone balancing. It is for both adults and children.

Sign up for our free newsletter and receive a free gift!

Send John Gray your favorite insights from *Why Mars and Venus Collide* or sign up for our free newsletter and receive a free updated e-book of answers to the most commonly asked questions he receives. Send your questions and feedback to JohnGray@marsvenus.com and receive in return a special Mars Venus e-book.

For additional information please call or write to:

John Gray Seminars
20 Sunnyside Avenue, Suite A-130
Mill Valley, CA 94941
1-877-JOHNGRAY (1-877-5646-4729)